$14⁹⁵

Recipes for
FAT FREE LIVING 4
COOKBOOK

FAT FREE
BREADS
FOR BREAD MACHINES

EVERY ~~I~~
UNDER 1 GR~~A~~ ~~T~~
PER SERVING

I0956782

<u>Recipes for FAT FREE LIVING COOKBOOK 4</u>
<u>BREADS</u>

Copyright 1996 by Fat Free Living, Inc.
First Printing 1996

All rights reserved. No portion of this book may be reproduced in any form without prior written permission of Fat Free Living, Inc.

Please consult your doctor with any personal questions about yourself and this book. Jyl Steinback and Fat Free Living, Inc. disclaim all liability in connection with the use of this book.

Front and Rear cover photos by
Elliot Lincus, Camel Studios

Front and Rear cover design by
Mark Nickel, Graphics 4

ISBN 0-9636876-5-4
Jyl Steinback
Fat Free Living, Inc.
15020 N. 50th Place
Scottsdale, Arizona 85254
602-996-6300

Printed by Jumbo Jack's Cookbooks • A Division of Audubon Media Corporation
1-800-798-2635

Acknowledgements

We've done it again, THANKS TO ALL OF YOU!!!

Our company FAT FREE LIVING, INC. and myself are blessed with a new full-time partner. This extremely special person in my life is my soulmate and very "bestest" friend and husband, Gary Steinback. LUCKY ME!!! Gary just joined FAT FREE LIVING, INC. April 1, 1996 and it was no joke, thank goodness. It was a moment we dreamed of for a long time and has finally become a wonderful reality. Gary, is an inspiration! He is self-motivating, persistent, a "wiz" at business, and fabulous at telling "corny" jokes that keep my sister Jacie laughing every time! I am the lucky one to have Gary in my life and everyday I am extremely thankful for the gift that we have...each other! Gar...it's going to be an awesome year, <u>together</u> we can make it happen! You're the BEST!!!

Two other very special people have also made this book possible and help make all my dreams reality, and that's my Mom and Dad, Betty and Bill Levy. My dad has tasted every bread he could. He said, "They're FAT FREE" and my mom kept saying, "that's enough Bill." Their wonderful support and love they have for each of their children, Jacie, myself, and Jeff, is extraordinary and we are all lucky to be so gifted by two wonderful and caring parents!

But, my two sensational children, Jamie and Scott, I want to give you both a great big kiss and lots of big hugs for how patient and "totally great" you both are always. In the last three months we've had FAT FREE corndogs, bageldogs, pizza, cinnamon rolls, blueberry bagels, white bread, whole wheat bread, a breadaholics dream, I'm not sure it was Jamie's and Scott's. But they never complained they just ate it and gave me their opinion. Always great, of course. I am so very lucky to have you both in my life and I thank my lucky stars everyday for both of you! Thanks, Jamie and Scott, you're the <u>best</u>, and you always make me smile!

Thanks A Million!!!

First, I want to thank all of you...yes you...that are reading this right now. Good for you for wanting a healthier lifestyle. Good for you for joining me on my mission for FAT FREE LIVING! I am grateful to you all! Thank you for making FAT FREE LIVING part of your life, for you are the perfect ingredient in helping make our world a healthier place.

This book would not be possible without the phenomenal support and limitless energy of the following people. Thanks a million!

Mikki Eveloff, we're at it again. Fifteen calls back and forth a day. Making bread after bread after bread. You are <u>incredible</u> and a blessing in my life. I love working with you, Mikki! I love your upbeat personality, positive motivation, and your wonderful gift to get things done...yesterday! Thanks a million!

Debra Kohl, I am not surprised we did it again! How lucky I am to have your positive personality and fabulous knowledge of nutrition with me again on another FAT FREE venture. Debra is a Registered Dietician with a master's degree in Nutrition and Dietetics and you can reach her sensational services at 266-0324. Tell her Jyl sent you and enjoy a healthier YOU! Thanks a million, Deb!

Elliot Luncis, you are a doll! Thanks for the beautiful sunset! Just exactly as I had visioned...YOU made it HAPPEN! The front and back covers are sensational! You outdid yourself and I appreciate every minute of your positive encouragement and outstanding energy! Thanks a million, Elliot, for being extraordinary!

Mark Nickel, I definitely couldn't do it without you. It seems every time I call you I tell you I need it yesterday and each and every time you come through with flying colors and then some! Not only did you help redesign the covers of Recipes for FAT FREE Living Cookbooks 1, 2 & 3 you have now made FAT FREE BREADS covers one of my favorites. You and your computer are amazing and I am extremely grateful to you both! Thank you a million. You are a gift in your field and in my life!

Mike Ruddy, a huge hug of thanks to you! You have helped FAT FREE Living, Inc. and myself in so many wonderful ways. Your energy is contagious and your precision to do a job right is a gift to any business. Mike is the Sales Manager to Jumbo Jack's Cookbooks who prints all 4 of my FAT FREE Living Cookbooks. I think you're GREAT! Thanks a million for EVERYTHING!

Terri Irwin, you're a doll! Thanks to you and Pottery Barn at the Biltmore Fashion Park our front and back covers are SPECTACULAR! An awesome job you did! Thanks a million for making it all possible, and for your wonderful generosity!

Brenda McLaughlin, community manager at San Antiqua on McCormick Ranch, made our background scenery an unbelievable sight! Thanks!

Recipes for FAT FREE LIVING Cookbook
SUCCESS STORIES

Dear Jyl,

I traveled from the East side to the West side of New Hampshire and into Vermont looking for your cookbooks. Needless to say I had no luck. My disappointment forced me to call you. Your <u>Recipes for FAT FREE Living Cookbooks</u> are the absolute best!!! Out with all the other cookbooks!

I plan on climbing the Grand Canyon in December and the only extra weight I plan on carrying is my backpack. Thank you for caring about us!

Beatice Laramie, Claremont, NH

❖   ❖   ❖

Dear Jyl,

As I shared with you on the phone, our family has lost over 80 pounds because of your FAT FREE Living Cookbooks. Our grandson, who is living with us until he gets his own apartment, has lost over 40 pounds. My husband has lost 20 pounds and I have lost 20 pounds.

We went from eating 60 to 80 grams of fat per day to eating less than 20 grams of fat per day and not feeling deprived. We have normal, attractive, tasty meals and are able to have a variety of foods. Because of this, we are not on a diet but we have made a lifestyle change that will be permanent.

My husband and I have tried every diet known. We have lost numerous pounds only to gain them back plus more. I am confident that we will continue to eat the same because we enjoy the recipes so much in your books and they taste normal.

Our grandson, who is 21 years old, is totally sold on FAT FREE Living. He has been watching when we prepare the recipes, since he is soon going to move into an apartment. When he first tasted the Mexican Layer Dip he said, "This is awesome! I am gonna learn how to make this!" We have made tacos using corn tortillas (fat-free) just by adding fresh lettuce to the dip after "nuking" it for 50 seconds.

All three of our daughters have purchased your books and are beginning to cook FAT FREE!

I am an RN who works in a CCU here in Billings. I have taken a few of your recipes to work to share with my colleagues. After tasting these marvelous treats, ex: Cherry Cheesecake and Mexican Layer Dip, many have become converts and have since gotten the <u>FAT FREE Living Cookbooks</u>. I even shared a slice of the Cherry Cheesecake with a patient who had just undergone angioplasty. He believed that changing his eating lifestyle <u>could be painless, after</u> tasting the cheesecake.

My husband has had 2 angioplasties 2 years ago. He is excited to see if by reducing his fat grams to 10% of his calorie intake, accompanied by a regular exercise program (he exercises daily at a local health club), that he can reverse some of his current blockage.

Thank you again, Jyl, for a new way of healthy, tasty, enjoyable, FAT FREE LIVING!

Mary Jo Hardy, Billings, MT

❖   ❖   ❖

Dear Jyl,

Thank you for all your great books. I love them!!!

Love, Lisa Hindy, Kaysville, UT

❖ ❖ ❖

Dear Jyl,

I just wanted to write you and update you on my progress since we last spoke. When I contacted you in March, I was about 10 pounds overweight with a body fat percentage of 26.5%. My daughter was just about to turn two, and I couldn't understand why 2 years after her birth I still felt so heavy! I tried several types of diets but nothing seemed to help - before I had my daughter I was firmer and felt better about myself. Although I was consistently weight training and doing aerobics, I was very discouraged until I spoke with you.

I started to make several of your recipes from <u>Recipes For FAT FREE Living Cookbook 1 and 2</u> and found them absolutely delicious! One recipe in particular, your Seafood Rice Casserole, was on our dinner table at least two times a week!!! (I would even eat it for leftovers for lunch and I even took it to the beach.) I also became much more aware of the amount of protein, fat and carbohydrates I was consuming.

By August, my body fat was down to 23% and I had dropped 5 pounds. When I called you last week my body fat was 21% and I had dropped another 5 pounds. At this point I am working now simply to reshape my body, stay at the same weight but build more muscle.

I would say the combination of weight-training 3 times a week, three 30-minute aerobic sessions a week and eating as FAT FREE as possible has really made the difference for me. Your enthusiasm really kept me going! What I admire so much about you is no matter how busy you are, you always take time out to return and respond to every call, and letter you receive.

I can't thank you enough for all of your encouragement!

Nancy L. Kruh-Meyer, Merrick, NY

❖ ❖ ❖

Dear Jyl,

I enjoy both of your cookbooks, use them a lot! We eat the fat-free cornbread almost every night. Keep up the great job.

Alice Walker, Virginia Beach, VA

❖ ❖ ❖

Dear Jyl,

I want to thank you for helping me change my eating habits. I love <u>Recipes for FAT FREE Living 1 and 2</u>. They have been a large part of my diet. Keep those books coming!

April DosSanto, Athens, GA

❖ ❖ ❖

Hi Jyl,

I received my FAT FREE COOKBOOKS from Dani Eveloff, a co-worker of mine. Since receiving her gift, I've been <u>most impressed</u> with the results of the many dishes I have tried. What Fun! As well as, <u>GREAT TASTE</u>!!! I'd like to give 2 gifts for the holiday - if you could rush this order, I'd appreciate it. Thanks and wishing you a healthy and blessed holiday.

Date Kennedy, Council Bluffs, IA

❖ ❖ ❖

Dear Jyl,

I love using your FAT FREE LIVING COOKBOOKS, because the recipes use ordinary ingredients, also everyone raves about the food and we <u>don't</u> even miss the fat! A real favorite is the Banana Brownie Sundae. Thanks again!

Sheryl Rykerd, Alpine, CA

Dear Jyl,

We love your cookbooks! Our daughter purchased <u>Recipes for FAT FREE Living Cookbooks</u> in St. Louis and I am ordering 2 copies for gifts.

My husband had 7 by-passes at age 47 and then a heart attack. We both eat FAT FREE following Dean Ornish's Reversing Heart Disease Plan. Your cookbooks are <u>very</u> helpful. Thank you!

Loretta Fingert, Des Moines, IA

Dear Jyl,

I recommend Jyl's <u>Recipes For FAT FREE Living Cookbooks, 1, 2 and 3</u> without reservation. Not only are they extremely healthy, but they are easy and taste great. As a physician who knows the massive importance of maintaining a low-fat lifestyle, I daily and devoutly recommend Jyl's books to any of my patients looking to lose weight and live a healthier lifestyle.

Dr. Gary Silverman, Author: FATT is a 4 letter word

Dear Jyl,

Greetings from Germany! We are planning to stay in Germany for perhaps another year or so. Anita has an opportunity to increase her exposure throughout the region. Just this past weekend she attended an annual fitness convention in Central Germany. She was able to introduce all three of your cookbooks there. Needless to say, they were a hit! The word is out about your FAT FREE Living cookbooks. We wanted to inform you of this to share some of our excitement for the future. We thank you so much for what you have done in creating these products and for working so well with us. Once again, THANK YOU!!!

L. Lee Acker III, Germany

Dear Jyl,

Thank your so much for sending me the "full" <u>Recipes Far FAT FREE Living Cookbook 2</u>. How thoughtful of you for going the extra mile in customer service.

I admire your energy to publish such excellent cookbooks, take care of a family, and find time to stay fit. My husband and I face similar challenges too…What fun!

Your fat free recipes have helped to keep us in shape (my husband, A.C., will be carrying the Olympic Torch in June).

Wishing you continued prosperity and a blessed eye for you and yours! Love, "Lynn"

Carolyn Robbins, Durham, NC

Nothing stimulates the senses quite like fresh baked bread. The crispy, golden brown outside perfectly complements the soft, tender texture of the inside. The lofting aroma of a crackling hot loaf conjures up visions of local bakers working the soft, malleable ball of dough into an artistic masterpiece. Just the thought can make your mouth water.

Bread products are a basic part of the meal in every country of the world. It may vary in shape and texture but the basic ingredients of flour and water are essential to balance a meal. Not only does bread taste and smell like a little piece of heaven, it also provides a very low-fat source of B vitamins, iron and fiber. It is relatively low in calories, depending on what you put on it, and it can be quite filling.

Bread gives pizazz to a plain, simple meal. It can be the source for rave reviews from your dinner guests and it is easier than ever to make. A product that used to take hours of hands-on work, takes little more than dumping in your favorite ingredients and flipping a switch, thanks to the ingenious invention of the bread machine. Equipped with a bread machine and a little creativity, even the most ungifted baker can turn out a gorgeous loaf of bread to tempt the most finicky palate.

The recipes in this book were analyzed using the Nutrients III and IV nutrient analysis program. Products not listed on the original data base were added using the nutrition facts section of the product label. All nutrients were rounded to the nearest whole number.

Debra Kohl, MS, RD

INTRODUCTION

Bread machine baking seems almost magical once you get the hang of it. It's fun, challenging, and creative with wonderful edible results! The successful fat-free bread baker needs five key ingredients: yeast, flour, sugar, liquid, and...PATIENCE! All the recipes in this book include ingredients to produce 1-pound or 1 1/2-pound loaves; the recipe you use depends on your machine.

KEYS TO SUCCESSFUL BREAD-BAKING

Fresh ingredients and precise measurements are essential to successful bread baking. The type of flour you use will affect the texture, density, and height of your bread. Bread flours produce a lighter, higher loaf than whole grain flours; these breads tend to be denser with a mealy texture. By varying the proportions or combining different flours you can create a wonderful array of flavors and textures. Always use clear measuring cups with easy-to-read measurements. Tap dry ingredients down and make sure the top is level. Place measuring cups with liquids on the counter and read carefully to assure accurate measurements. Standard measuring spoons are the only accurate way to measure small exact quantities as yeast, salt, or sweeteners. Tableware spoons vary and will not measure accurately. A heaping cup of flour or a table teaspoon of yeast can create a disaster from the most perfect recipe.

INGREDIENTS

1. **WHITE FLOUR** - Bread flour (we prefer Gold Medal or Pillsbury) produces a higher loaf of bread than all-purpose flour because it has a higher gluten content. All-purpose flour can be used for sweet doughs, dinner rolls, or breads that do not need to rise as high, but we still prefer the results when using bread flour.

2. **WHOLE WHEAT FLOUR** - Whole wheat flours produce a much denser loaf than white flour because it has a lower gluten content. We found the most appealing wheat breads to be made with a combination of white and wheat flours. If you want to try the recipes with only whole wheat flour, you will need to add more yeast; this is where a little creativity and patience come into play.

3. **RYE FLOUR** - Rye flour will not rise well when used by itself. It is best combined with a higher gluten flour to produce wonderful Pumpernickel, Raisin Rye, and other dark breads. These are usually denser loaves and will not rise as high as breads made solely with white flour.

4. **CORNMEAL** - Yellow and white cornmeal are interchangeable in any of the recipes requiring cornmeal. Cornmeal is always combined with higher gluten flours; cornbreads have a slightly sweet flavor and more crumbly texture.

There are numerous types of flours available at health food and specialty stores, but our recipes were developed by using the most readily available flours (bread flour, whole wheat, all-purpose, rye, and cornmeal).

5. **OATMEAL** - Oatmeal is always combined with other flours because it does not contain any gluten. Most of the recipes recommend multi-grain oatmeal (Quaker Oats) because it has a lower fat content than regular oats. You can substitute any "rolled" or "old-fashioned" oats, but do not use instant oatmeal. Regular oats will affect the nutritional value of the bread, but not significantly.

6. **YEAST** - Yeast is very sensitive and requires certain key ingredients to activate it properly. Sugars make yeast grow and salt slows it down; hot water will kill yeast and cold water will keep if from reactivating. Always use fresh yeast, as expired yeast will create an inedible, flat, hard bread. Store yeast in the refrigerator and it will stay fresh until the expiration date printed on the package. There are a variety of yeasts available on the market; we found the best results with Fleischmann's yeast for the bread machine. The recipes in this book were tested with several different types of active dry or rapid-rise yeasts, but the results were most consistent when using yeast for the bread machine.

7. **LIQUIDS** - Any liquids (water, milk, etc.) must be warm (100 to 110 degrees F) to activate the yeast. Hot tap water usually works fine; milk can be easily warmed in the microwave on HIGH for 15 to 30 seconds (depending on the required amount). Do not overheat the milk or water - you will KILL the yeast! We chose all low-fat products (skim milk, nonfat dry milk powder with water, etc.) to create wonderful fat-free breads. Any liquids can be substituted (1%, 2%, whole milk for skim milk) but will alter the nutritional content of the bread (higher calories and fat).

8. **EGGS** - In order to produce fat-free breads we have used egg whites or fat-free egg substitutes with wonderful results. 2 egg whites is equivalent to 1/4 cup egg substitute; you can successfully substitute these for one another. Using whole eggs (1 egg = 2 egg whites or 1/4 cup egg substitute) will increase the fat and caloric content.

9. **FAT SUBSTITUTES** - You will not find any butter or oil in any of the recipes in this book. We used a variety of products that are readily available to create deliciously light, fat-free breads. Applesauce (lite applesauce is recommended for reduced-calorie content), Lighter Bake (substitute 1st stage baby food prune purée if this product is not available in your area), apple butter (preferably unsweetened), fat-free margarine (Promise), nonfat yogurt, and nonfat sour cream have replaced fatty butter and fats to create guilt-free, fat-free breads.

10. **SALT** - Salt is necessary in most recipes because it inhibits the yeast. We have used a minimal amount of salt in all the recipes, but if you are on a salt-restricted diet, try reducing or eliminating the salt. The rise and texture of the bread will be affected; most commonly, the bread will tend to rise too high and then collapse. Salt substitutes are not effective as a replacement because they do not contain the yeast-inhibiting properties of real salt.

11. **SWEETENERS-** A little bit of sugar goes a long way in that loaf of bread. Sweeteners activate the yeast to create beautifully high loaves, as well as contributing to the flavor, color and texture of the bread. White sugar and brown sugar can be substituted for one another in equal amounts. You can also substitute honey, molasses, or maple syrup for any sweeteners, but you need to slightly reduce the liquid content for accurate results. If you are on a sugar-restricted diet, try reducing the sugar to 1/2 to 1 teaspoon. Eliminating the sugar will work better in some recipes than others; remember, PATIENCE is one of the key ingredients to successful bread baking. Do not use aspartame as a sugar substitute, as it does not interact with the yeast.

12. **SPICES** - For the best flavor, always use fresh or dried spices that have been stored properly. Dried herbs can be substituted for any fresh herbs (1 tablespoon fresh herbs = 1 teaspoon crushed dried herbs - 1/2 teaspoon ground herbs). If a certain spice or herb does not appeal to you, either eliminate it or replace it with a more desirable choice.

13. **ADDITIONAL INGREDIENTS** - Fresh and dried fruits are very often added to the bread recipe. Although most bread machine manufacturers recommend adding these ingredients during the raisin-bread cycle, or 5 minutes before the end of the kneading cycle, our results were just as successful when these ingredients were tossed right in at the beginning. If you do not want to wait around for the kneading

cycle to end, try tossing those fruits right in; this should not affect the bread, but the fruits may be more finely chopped. To keep the fat content down, we used Grape-Nuts or nonfat granola to add extra crunch instead of fatty nuts. Health-Valley granola tends to be somewhat heavier than lighter granolas and may create a heavier, denser loaf of bread. Fat-free Millstone Bakery granolas are available in a variety of flavors. These are usually sold in health food or specialty stores. Grated fruit rinds come from the colored portion of the fruit. Use a vegetable peeler to remove only the outer rind (zest) and avoid the bitter part (pith) underneath. Fruit rinds blend best when added with other liquid ingredients.

PROBLEM-SOLVING

1. "A TOTAL FAILURE" - This is usually caused by inaccurate measurements, missing ingredients, or improper settings for baking. Line your ingredients up in the order they need to be added and use <u>accurate</u> measuring utensil: NO MORE FAILURES!

2. "HIGH TO LOW LOAVES" - The size and appearance of bread loaves will vary, depending on the ingredients. Breads made with white bread flour are lighter and higher than those made with whole wheat or rye flours; these tend to be denser and darker, but the flavor should not be affected.

3. "FLAT LOAVES" - Failure to rise can be caused by several factors which include:
   a. too much low-gluten flour (rye, whole wheat, etc.).
   b. too little sugar which feeds the yeast and promotes rising.
   c. too much salt which inhibits the activation of the yeast.
   d. expired yeast which will not activate even if all other ingredients are perfect.
   e. hot liquids which will kill the yeast or cold liquids that will not activate the yeast; stick to liquid temperatures that range from 100 to 110 degrees F.

4. "OVER-THE-TOP LOAF" - If your loaf rises too high and sticks to the top of the machine it is usually caused by:
   a. too much yeast.
   b. too much liquid - if you are replacing white or brown sugar with honey, molasses, or maple syrup, reduce the liquid 1 teaspoon for every 5 teaspoons of sweetener.
   c. too much sugar; watch out for extra sugar in dried fruits, sweetened apple butters, etc.

5. **"RISE AND FALL LOAVES"** - Some breads will rise beautifully and suddenly collapse in the center after baking. This can usually be attributed to:

   a. not enough salt - We were able to reduce salt to 1/2 to 3/4 teaspoon in most recipes (1 - 1 1/2 pound, respectively) without significant changes in results.

   b. too much liquid - Fruits and vegetables add extra moisture to the bread, so you may need to reduce the liquid content slightly.

6. **"CRUMBLY DOUGH"** - Too much flour is the simple explanation. This can be resolved by adding a little more liquid 1 tablespoon at a time. Make sure you allow the liquid to mix in before adding any more.

7. **"STICKY DOUGH"** - Too much liquid is the simple explanation. When extra-moist ingredients as applesauce, honey, yogurt, sour cream, etc., are added, you may need to reduce the water accordingly or slightly increase the amount of flour (1 tablespoon at a time). Some bagel or sweet doughs may seem too sticky when they are removed from the machine, but you can solve this problem by lightly kneading the dough on a floured surface before the second rise.

8. **"SOGGY CRUST"** - Remove the bread from the machine as soon as possible and cool at room temperature on a rack. Cooling too long in the machine can create soggy crusts. Allow the bread to cool to room temperature before slicing or storing.

9. **"HARD-AS-ROCK FLAT LOAVES"** - Three factors may contribute to hard, flat, squatty loaves of bread.

   a. forgotten or inactive yeast - Lining up your ingredients in the order they need to be added can usually reduce the chance of forgotten ingredients. Make sure you use yeast that has not expired and has been stored properly.

   b. too hot or too cold liquid - Remember that hot water kills the yeast and cold water keeps it inactive. Ideal temperature is 100 to 110 degrees F.

   c. too much salt will inhibit the activity of the yeast.

ADDITIONAL HINTS FOR THAT PERFECT LOAF OF BREAD

1. Any of these recipes can be baked in the oven. Remove dough after the dough cycle and let rise in a warm place until doubled in size, about 45 minutes to 1 hour. Shape loaves on baking sheet or place in a loaf pan (9x5 for 1 1/2-pound recipes; 8x4 for 1-pound recipe) and bake in preheated 375 degree oven for 35 to 45 minutes, until lightly browned.

2. Determine the bread setting according to the instructions in your manual. Most of the breads tested produced successful results on the Rapid-bake cycle. Whole wheat, Pumpernickel, and Rye breads may require a longer cycle for optimum results.

3. Bread dough can be stored in the refrigerator (1 to 2 days) or freezer (up to 1 month) if you do not want to bake it right away. Refrigerated dough should be brought to room temperature, covered ,and rise in a warm place until doubled in size before baking. Frozen dough must be thoroughly defrosted, covered, and rise until doubled in size before baking.

4. Cool bread completely before storing. Wrap in plastic, foil or plastic storage bags; bread will stay fresh in the refrigerator up to 1 week or in the freezer for one month. For easy toasting, slice bread before freezing, and toast straight from the freezer.

5. Use these measurement equivalents for simple conversions:
   1 1/2 tsp. = 1/2 tbsp.
   3 tsp. = 1 tbsp.
   4 tbsp. = 1/4 cup
   5 1/3 tbsp. = 1/3 cup
   2 tbsp. = 1/8 cup
   16 tbsp. = 1 cup
   1/4 cup + 2 tbsp. = 3/8 cup
   1/2 cup + 2 tbsp. = 5/8 cup
   3/4 cup + 2 tbsp. = 7/8 cup
   1 cup + 2 tbsp. = 1 1/8 cups

6. **HAVE FUN** - Experiment with flours, spices, fruit and other ingredients that appeal to you. Once you determine the best combination of ingredients for your machine, almost anything is possible. Enjoy the enticing aroma of fresh-baked bread everyday - as simple as 1...2...3!!!

There are several new bread machines on the market that bake 1-, 1 1/2-, and 2-pound loaves of bread. To the best of our knowledge from simple testing, most 1-pound recipes can be doubled to bake a perfect 2-pound loaf. As with any bread recipe, trial and error is the answer and PATIENCE is the key. Refer to "Problem Solving" for simple solutions.

FAT-FREE
BEAUTIFUL BREADS
FOR BREAD MACHINES

BEAUTIFUL
BREADS

ALMOND WHEAT BREAD

1-POUND RECIPE (8 SLICES)

ingredients:
1 tsp. yeast
1/2 tsp. salt
1 1/3 cups bread flour
1/3 cup whole-wheat flour
1 tbsp. brown sugar
1/4 tsp. almond extract
3 oz. skim milk, warmed
1/4 cup water

1 1/2-POUND RECIPE (12 SLICES)

ingredients:
1 1/2 tsp. yeast
3/4 tsp. salt
2 cups bread flour
1/2 cup whole wheat flour
1 1/2 tbsp. brown sugar
1/4 tsp. almond extract
1/2 cup skim milk, warmed
1/2 cup water

directions:
Add ingredients in the order suggested by the bread machine manufacturer and follow baking instructions provided in the manual.

Nutrition per Serving	1-Pound	1 1/2-Pound
Calories	96	96
Carbohydrate	19 grams	19 grams
Cholesterol	< 1 milligram	< 1 milligram
Dietary Fiber	2 grams	2 grams
Protein	4 grams	4 grams
Sodium	141 milligrams	141 milligrams

Exchanges

	1 1/3 starch	1 1/3 starch

APPLE BREAD

1-POUND RECIPE (8 SLICES)

ingredients: 1 tsp. yeast
1/4 tsp. salt
1 tbsp. nonfat dry milk
1 tsp. cinnamon
3/4 tsp. nutmeg
2 1/2 cups bread flour
2 tbsp. lite applesauce
2/3 cup water
1/2 cup dried apples, chopped

1 1/2-POUND RECIPE (12 SLICES)

ingredients: 1 1/2 tsp. yeast
1/2 tsp. salt
2 tbsp. nonfat dry milk
2 tsp. cinnamon
1 tsp. nutmeg
3 1/3 cups bread flour
3 T. lite applesauce
1 cup water
3/4 cup dried apples, chopped

directions: Add ingredients in the order suggested by the bread machine manufacturer and follow baking instructions provided in the manual.

Nutrition per Serving	1-Pound	1 1/2-Pound
Calories	146	133
Carbohydrate	30 grams	27 grams
Cholesterol	0 milligrams	0 milligrams
Dietary Fiber	2 grams	2 grams
Protein	4 grams	4 grams
Sodium	77 milligrams	100 milligrams

Exchanges

	1 1/3 starch	1 1/3 starch
	2/3 fruit	1/2 fruit

2

APPLE-CRANBERRY BREAD

1-POUND RECIPE (8 SLICES)

ingredients:
1 1/2 tsp. yeast
1/2 tsp. salt
2 1/2 cups bread flour
1/2 cup multi-grain oatmeal
1 1/2 tsp. cinnamon
3 tbsp. molasses
2 tbsp. apple butter
1 cup water
1/2 cup diced apple
1/2 cup cranberry

1 1/2-POUND RECIPE (12 SLICES)

ingredients:
2 1/2 tsp. yeast
3/4 tsp. salt
3 1/3 cups bread flour
2/3 cup multi-grain oatmeal
2 tsp. cinnamon
1/4 cup molasses
3 tbsp. apple butter
1 1/3 cups water
3/4 cup diced apple
3/4 cup cranberry

directions: Add ingredients in the order suggested by the bread machine manufacturer and follow baking instructions provided in the manual.

Nutrition per Serving	1-Pound	1 1/2-Pound
Calories	206	188
Carbohydrate	45 grams	41 grams
Cholesterol	0 milligrams	0 milligrams
Dietary Fiber	3 grams	3 grams
Protein	6 grams	5 grams
Sodium	140 milligrams	139 milligrams

Exchanges

	1-Pound	1 1/2-Pound
	2 starch	1 2/3 starch
	1 fruit	1 fruit

3

APPLE-GRANOLA BREAD

ingredients:
1-POUND RECIPE (8 SLICES)
1 1/4 tsp. yeast
1/2 tsp. salt
3/4 tsp. cinnamon
1/4 cup nonfat dry milk powder
1 tbsp. brown sugar
2 1/4 cups bread flour
1/2 cup nonfat granola
1 tbsp. apple butter
1/3 cup lite applesauce
2/3 cup water

ingredients:
1 1/2-POUND RECIPE (12 SLICES)
1 3/4 tsp. yeast
1 tsp. salt
1 1/4 tsp. cinnamon
1/3 cup nonfat dry milk powder
2 tbsp. brown sugar
2 3/4 cups bread flour
3/4 cup nonfat granola
2 tbsp. apple butter
1/2 cup lite applesauce
1 cup water

directions: Add ingredients in the order suggested by the bread machine manufacturer and follow baking instructions provided in the manual.

Nutrition per Serving	1-Pound	1 1/2-Pound
Calories	156	138
Carbohydrate	32 milligrams	29 milligrams
Cholesterol	<1 milligram	< 1 milligram
Dietary Fiber	1 gram	1 gram
Protein	5 grams	4 grams
Sodium	149 milligrams	192 milligrams

Exchanges

	1-Pound	1 1/2-Pound
	2 starch	1 3/4 starch

APPLE-RAISIN-OAT BREAD

1-POUND RECIPE (8 SLICES)

ingredients:
1 1/2 tsp. yeast
1/2 tsp. salt
1 1/2 tsp. cinnamon
2 1/2 cups bread flour
1/2 cup multi-grain oatmeal
3 tbsp. molasses
2 tbsp. lite applesauce
1 cup water
1/2 cup diced apple
1/2 cup raisins

1 1/2-POUND RECIPE (12 SLICES)

ingredients:
2 1/2 tsp. yeast
3/4 tsp. salt
1 3/4 tsp. cinnamon
3 1/3 cups bread flour
2/3 cup multi-grain oatmeal
1/4 cup molasses
3 tbsp. lite applesauce
1 1/3 cups water
2/3 cup diced apple
3/4 cup raisins

directions: Add ingredients in the order suggested by the bread machine manufacturer and follow baking instructions provided in the manual.

Nutrition per Serving	1-Pound	1 1/2-Pound
Calories	198	180
Carbohydrate	43 grams	39 grams
Cholesterol	0 milligrams	0 milligrams
Dietary Fiber	3 grams	3 grams
Protein	6 grams	5 grams
Sodium	142 milligrams	138 milligrams

Exchanges

	1-Pound	1 1/2-Pound
	2 starch	1 2/3 starch
	2/3 fruit	1 fruit

APPLESAUCE BREAD

ingredients:

1-POUND RECIPE (8 SLICES)
1 tsp. yeast
3/4 tsp. salt
1 tbsp. brown sugar
1/2 cup Grape-Nuts
2 cups bread flour
2 tsp. frozen apple juice concentrate, thawed
1/4 cup lite applesauce
2/3 cup water

ingredients:

1 1/2-POUND RECIPE (12 SLICES)
1 1/2 tsp. yeast
1 tsp. salt
2 tbsp. brown sugar
2/3 cup Grape-Nuts
3 cups bread flour
1 tbsp. frozen apple juice concentrate, thawed
1/3 cup lite applesauce
3/4 cup + 2 tbsp. water

directions: Add ingredients in the order suggested by the bread machine manufacturer and follow baking instructions provided in the manual.

Nutrition per Serving	1-Pound	1 1/2-Pound
Calories	142	138
Carbohydrate	29 grams	29 grams
Cholesterol	0 milligrams	0 milligrams
Dietary Fiber	2 grams	2 grams
Protein	5 grams	4 grams
Sodium	253 milligrams	225 milligrams

APPLE STRUDEL

ingredients: **1-POUND RECIPE**
1 1/2 tsp. yeast
1/2 tsp. salt
2 cups + 1 tbsp. flour, divided
1/4 cup + 2 tbsp. sugar, divided
1/4 cup egg substitute
1/2 cup lite applesauce
1/2 cup skim milk
1 1/2 tbsp. fat-free margarine, melted
2 cups canned apple slices
1/3 cup brown sugar
1 1/2 tsp. cinnamon, divided
1/3 cup raisins

ingredients: **1 1/2-POUND RECIPE**
2 tsp. yeast
3/4 tsp. salt
3 cups + 1 1/2 tbsp. flour, divided
1/3 cup + 3 tbsp. sugar, divided
1/2 cup egg substitute
3/4 cup lite applesauce
1/2 cup skim milk
2 tbsp. fat-free margarine, melted
3 cups canned apple slices
1/2 cup brown sugar
2 tsp. cinnamon, divided
1/2 cup raisins

directions: Add yeast, salt, 1/4 or 1/3 cup sugar (depending on recipe size), 2 or 3 cups flour, egg substitute, lite applesauce, and milk in order recommended by bread machine manufacturer and process on dough cycle. Remove dough from pan; place on lightly-floured surface. Roll dough into 1 large or 2 small rectangles. Spread dough with melted margarine; sprinkle with apples, 1 or 1 1/2 tablespoons flour, brown sugar, 1 or 1 1/2 teaspoons cinnamon, and raisins. Roll up dough lengthwise; pinch edges together to seal. Lightly spray large baking sheet (with edges) or 10x15x1-inch jellyroll pan with nonfat cooking spray. Place seam-side down on prepared pan. Cover; let rise 45 minutes, until doubled in size. In small bowl, combine remaining sugar and cinnamon; mix well. Sprinkle cinnamon-sugar on top of rolled dough. Preheat oven to 350 degrees. Bake in preheated oven 35 to 40 minutes, until lightly browned. Cool to room temperature before serving.

Nutrition per Serving	1-Pound	1 1/2-Pound
Calories	31	29
Carbohydrate	52 grams	50 grams
Cholesterol	< 1 milligram	< 1 milligram
Dietary Fiber	3 grams	3 grams
Protein	6 grams	5 grams
Sodium	176 milligrams	175 milligrams
Exchanges	2 starch	2 starch
	1 1/3 fruit	1 1/3 fruit

APRICOT-CRAISIN BREAD

1-POUND RECIPE (8 SLICES)

ingredients: 1 1/2 tsp. yeast
1/2 tsp. salt
2 tbsp. nonfat dry milk powder
2 1/4 cups bread flour
1/2 tsp. sugar
1 cup water
1/4 cup apricots, chopped
1/4 cup craisins
3 tbsp. applesauce
1/2 tsp. cinnamon

1 1/2 POUND-RECIPE (12 SLICES)

ingredients: 2 1/2 tsp. yeast
1 tsp. salt
3 tbsp. nonfat dry milk powder
3 1/4 cups bread flour
1 tbsp. sugar
1 1/2 cups water
1/3 cup apricots, chopped
1/3 cup craisins
4 tbsp. applesauce
3/4 tsp. cinnamon

directions: Add ingredients in the order suggested by the bread machine manufacturer and follow baking instructions provided in the manual.

Nutrition per Serving	1-Pound	1 1/2-Pound
Calories	139	133
Carbohydrate	28 grams	27 grams
Cholesterol	< 1 milligrams	< 1 milligrams
Dietary Fiber	2 grams	2 grams
Protein	5 grams	4 grams
Sodium	142 milligrams	183 milligrams

Exchanges

	1-Pound	1 1/2-Pound
	1 2/3 starch	1 1/3 starch
	1/4 fruit	1/2 fruit

APRICOT-OATMEAL BREAD

1-POUND RECIPE (8 SLICES)

ingredients:
1 1/2 tsp. yeast
3/4 tsp. salt
2 tbsp. nonfat dry milk powder
1/2 cup multi-grain oatmeal
1 cup whole wheat flour
1 1/2 cups bread flour
1 tbsp. sugar
2 tbsp. peach butter
1 cup water
1/3 cup dried apricots, chopped

1 1/2-POUND RECIPE (12 SLICES)

ingredients:
2 1/2 tsp. yeast
1 tsp. salt
3 tbsp. nonfat dry milk powder
3/4 cup multi-grain oatmeal
1 1/4 cups whole wheat flour
2 cups bread flour
1 1/2 tbsp. sugar
3 tbsp. peach butter
1 1/4 cups water
3/4 cup dried apricots, chopped

directions: Add ingredients in the order suggested by the bread machine manufacturer and follow instructions provided in the manual.

Nutrition per Serving	1-Pound	1 1/2-Pound
Calories	128	168
Carbohydrate	38 grams	36 grams
Cholesterol	< 1 milligram	< 1 milligram
Dietary Fiber	4 grams	4 grams
Protein	6 grams	6 grams
Sodium	210 milligrams	188 milligrams

Exchanges

	1-Pound	1 1/2-Pound
	2 starch	2 starch
	1/4 fruit	1/4 fruit

BAKED PRETZELS

8 PRETZELS

ingredients:
1 1/2 tsp. yeast
1/2 tsp. salt
2 cups bread flour
1/2 cup egg substitute
1/4 cup water
1 egg white
1 tbsp. water

directions:
Add yeast, salt, bread flour, egg substitute, and 1/2 cup water in the order suggested by the bread machine manufacturer and process on the dough cycle. Preheat oven to 350 degrees. Lightly spray baking sheet with nonfat cooking spray. When the dough cycle is complete, remove dough and place on lightly-floured surface. Roll dough into 12x4-inch rectangle and cut into 8 (12-inch) strips. Pull each strip to about 14-inches in length. Form dough into pretzel shape: Make a circle; cross the ends at the top, twist the ends once and lay over the bottom of the circle. Pretzel logs can also be shaped just by making rolled dough into a 12- to 14-inch rope. Place pretzels on prepared baking sheet. In a small bowl, combine egg white with 1 tablespoon water and brush on pretzels. If desired, sprinkle pretzels with coarse salt, sesame, or poppy seeds. Bake in preheated oven 15 to 20 minutes, until lightly browned. Pretzels are best if served immediately or reheated in microwave on high 15 to 20 seconds. Serve with mustard or cheese dip.

Nutrition per Serving

Calories	111
Carbohydrate	20 grams
Cholesterol	0 milligrams
Dietary Fiber	1 gram
Protein	5 grams
Sodium	163 milligrams

Exchanges

1 1/2 starch

BANANA-BERRY BREAD

1-POUND RECIPE (8 SLICES)

ingredients:
- 1 1/2 tsp. yeast
- 3/4 tsp. salt
- 2 cups bread flour
- 2 tsp. brown sugar
- 1/3 cup nonfat banana yogurt
- 2 tbsp. lite applesauce
- 1/2 cup water
- 1/2 cup craisins

1 1/2-POUND RECIPE (12 SLICES)

ingredients:
- 2 tsp. yeast
- 1 tsp. salt
- 3 cups bread flour
- 1 tbsp. brown sugar
- 1/2 cup nonfat banana yogurt
- 1/4 cup lite applesauce
- 3/4 cup water
- 3/4 cup craisins

directions:
Add ingredients in the order suggested by the bread machine manufacturer and follow baking instructions provided in the manual.

Nutrition per Serving	1-Pound	1 1/2-Pound
Calories	138	138
Carbohydrate	29 grams	29 grams
Cholesterol	< 1 milligram	< 1 milligram
Dietary Fiber	2 grams	2 grams
Protein	4 grams	4 grams
Sodium	187 milligrams	210 milligrams

Exchanges

	1-Pound	1 1/2-Pound
	1 1/3 starch	1 1/3 starch
	2/3 fruit	2/3 fruit

BANANA BREAD

1-POUND RECIPE (8 SLICES)

ingredients:
1 tsp. yeast
1/2 tsp. salt
1 tsp. sugar
1 tbsp. nonfat dry milk powder
1/2 tsp. cinnamon
2 1/4 cups bread flour
3/4 cup mashed bananas
3 tbsp. lite applesauce
3/4 cup water

1 1/2-POUND RECIPE (12 SLICES)

ingredients:
2 tsp. yeast
3/4 tsp. salt
2 tsp. sugar
2 tbsp. nonfat dry milk powder
1 tsp. cinnamon
3 1/3 cups bread flour
1 cup mashed bananas
4 tbsp. lite applesauce
1 cup water

directions: Add ingredients in the order suggested by the bread machine manufacturer and follow baking instructions provided in the manual.

Nutrition per Serving	1-Pound	1 1/2-Pound
Calories	132	131
Carbohydrate	27 grams	27 grams
Cholesterol	< 1 milligram	< 1 milligram
Dietary Fiber	2 grams	2 grams
Protein	4 grams	5 grams
Sodium	139 milligrams	140 milligrams

Exchanges

	1 1/3 starch	1 1/3 starch
	1/3 fruit	1/3 fruit

BANANA-CRANBERRY BREAD

ingredients: **1-POUND RECIPE (8 SLICES)**
1 1/2 tsp. yeast
3/4 tsp. salt
1 tsp. cinnamon
3/4 cup multi-grain oatmeal
2 1/4 cups bread flour
3 tbsp. molasses
2 tbsp. lite applesauce
1/4 cup egg substitute
3/4 cup mashed bananas
3/4 cup water
1/4 cup dried cranberries

ingredients: **1 1/2-POUND RECIPE (12 SLICES)**
2 1/2 tsp. yeast
1 tsp. salt
1 1/2 tsp. cinnamon
1 cup multi-grain oatmeal
3 cups bread flour
1/4 cup molasses
3 tbsp. lite applesauce
1/4 cup egg substitute
1 egg white
1 cup mashed bananas
1 cup water
1/2 cup dried cranberries

directions: Add ingredients in the order suggested by the bread machine manufacturer and follow instructions provided in the manual.

Nutrition per Serving	1-Pound	1 1/2-Pound
Calories	177	158
Carbohydrate	37 grams	33 grams
Cholesterol	0 milligrams	0 milligrams
Dietary Fiber	3 grams	3 grams
Protein	6 grams	5 grams
Sodium	216 milligrams	190 milligrams

Exchanges		
	2 starch	1 2/3 starch
	1/2 fruit	1/2 fruit

13

BANANA-DATE BREAD

1-POUND RECIPE (8 SLICES)

ingredients:
1 1/4 tsp. yeast
1/4 tsp. salt
1 1/2 cups bread flour
3/4 cups whole wheat flour
3/4 cup water
1/4 cup mashed bananas
1/4 cup chopped dates

1 1/2-POUND RECIPE (12 SLICES)

ingredients:
2 tsp. yeast
1/2 tsp. salt
2 3/4 cups bread flour
2/3 cup whole wheat flour
1 cup + 2 tbsp. water
1/3 cup mashed bananas
1/3 cup chopped dates

directions: Add ingredients in the order suggested by the bread machine manufacturer and follow baking instructions provided in the manual.

Nutrition per Serving	1-Pound	1 1/2-Pound
Calories	134	134
Carbohydrate	28 grams	28 grams
Cholesterol	0 milligrams	0 milligrams
Dietary Fiber	3 grams	3 grams
Protein	5 grams	5 grams
Sodium	91 milligrams	91 milligrams

Exchanges

	1 3/4 starch	1 3/4 starch

BANANA-OAT BREAD

1-POUND RECIPE (8 SLICES)

ingredients:
1 1/2 tsp. yeast
3/4 tsp. salt
1 tsp. cinnamon
3/4 cup multi-grain oatmeal
2 1/4 cups bread flour
3 tbsp. molasses
2 tbsp. frozen apple juice concentrate, thawed
1/4 cup egg substitute
1 cup mashed bananas

1 1/2-POUND RECIPE (12 SLICES)

ingredients:
2 1/2 tsp. yeast
1 tsp. salt
1 1/2 tsp. cinnamon
1 cup multi-grain oatmeal
3 cups bread flour
1/4 cup molasses
3 tbsp. frozen apple juice concentrate, thawed
1/4 cup egg substitute
1 egg white
1 1/4 cups mashed bananas

directions: Add ingredients in the order suggested by the bread machine manufacturer and follow instructions provided in the manual.

Nutrition per Serving	1-Pound	1 1/2-Pound
Calories	180	165
Carbohydrate	38 grams	35 grams
Cholesterol	0 milligrams	0 milligrams
Dietary Fiber	3 grams	3 grams
Protein	6 grams	6 grams
Sodium	217 milligrams	195 milligrams

Exchanges

	1-Pound	1 1/2-Pound
	2 starch	2 starch
	1/3 fruit	1/4 fruit

BASIC WHITE BREAD

	1-POUND RECIPE (8 SLICES)
ingredients:	1 1/2 tsp. yeast
	3/4 tsp. salt
	2 1/2 cups bread flour
	2 tbsp. sugar
	2 tbsp. lite applesauce
	3/4 cup skim milk

	1 1/2-POUND RECIPE (12 SLICES)
ingredients:	2 1/2 tsp. yeast
	1 tsp. salt
	3 1/3 cups bread flour
	3 tbsp. sugar
	2 1/2 tbsp. lite applesauce
	1 cup skim milk

directions: Add ingredients in the order suggested by the bread machine manufacturer and follow instructions provided in the manual.

Nutrition per Serving	1-Pound	1 1/2-Pound
Calories	150	135
Carbohydrate	30 grams	27 grams
Cholesterol	0 milligrams	0 milligrams
Dietary Fiber	2 grams	2 grams
Protein	6 grams	5 grams
Sodium	215 milligrams	191 milligrams

Exchanges

	2 starch	1 3/4 starch

BLUEBERRY-ORANGE LOAF

1-POUND RECIPE (8 SLICES)

ingredients:
1 1/4 tsp. yeast
3/4 tsp. salt
1 tbsp. nonfat dry milk powder
2 tbsp. sugar
2 cups bread flour
1 tbsp. frozen orange juice concentrate, thawed
1 tsp. grated orange peel
3/4 cup water
1/4 cup dried blueberries

1 1/2-POUND RECIPE (12 SLICES)

ingredients:
2 tsp. yeast
1 1/4 tsp. salt
2 tbsp. nonfat dry milk powder
3 tbsp. sugar
3 cups flour
2 tbsp. frozen orange juice concentrate, thawed
1 1/2 tsp. grated orange peel
1 cup + 1 tbsp. water
1/3 cup dried blueberries

directions:
Add ingredients in the order suggested by the bread machine manufacturer and follow baking instructions provided in the manual.

Nutrition per Serving	1-Pound	1 1/2-Pound
Calories	125	127
Carbohydrate	26 grams	26 grams
Cholesterol	< 1 milligram	< 1 milligram
Dietary Fiber	2 grams	2 grams
Protein	4 grams	4 grams
Sodium	206 milligrams	232 milligrams

Exchanges

	1 1/2 starch	1 1/2 starch

BOSTON BROWN BREAD

1-POUND RECIPE (8 SLICES)

ingredients: 2 tsp. yeast
1/2 tsp. salt
2 tbsp. nonfat dry milk powder
1 tbsp. unsweetened cocoa powder
2 cups bread flour
1/2 cup whole wheat flour
1/2 cup rye flour
3 tbsp. molasses
3 tbsp. Lighter Bake
1 cup water
1/2 cup raisins

1 1/2-POUND RECIPE (12 SLICES)

ingredients: 2 1/2 tsp. yeast
3/4 tsp. salt
3 tbsp. nonfat dry milk powder
1 1/2 tbsp. unsweetened cocoa powder
2 1/3 cups bread flour
1/3 cup whole wheat flour
2/3 cup rye flour
1/4 cup molasses
1/4 cup Lighter Bake
1 1/3 cups water
1 cup raisins

directions: Add ingredients in the order suggested by the bread machine manufacturer and follow instructions provided in the manual.

Nutrition per Serving	1-Pound	1 1/2-Pound
Calories	243	205
Carbohydrate	53 grams	46 grams
Cholesterol	< 1 milligram	< 1 milligram
Dietary Fiber	3 grams	3 grams
Protein	6 grams	5 grams
Sodium	156 milligrams	154 milligrams

Exchanges

	1-Pound	1 1/2-Pound
	2 starch	2 starch
	1 1/2 fruit	1 fruit

BRAN BREAD

1-POUND RECIPE (8 SLICES)

ingredients:
1 1/2 tsp. yeast
1 tsp. salt
1 tbsp. nonfat dry milk powder
1 cup 100% Bran cereal
2 cups bread flour
2 tbsp. Lighter Bake
2 tbsp. honey
1 cup skim milk

1 1/2-POUND RECIPE (12 SLICES)

ingredients:
2 1/2 tsp. yeast
1 1/2 tsp. salt
2 tbsp. nonfat dry milk powder
1 1/3 cups 100% Bran cereal
2 2/3 cups bread flour
3 tbsp. Lighter Bake
3 tbsp. honey
1 1/3 cups skim milk

directions:
Add ingredients in the order suggested by the bread machine manufacturer and follow baking instructions provided in the manual.

Nutrition per Serving	1-Pound	1 1/2-Pound
Calories	164	150
Carbohydrate	35 grams	32 grams
Cholesterol	< 1 milligram	< 1 milligram
Dietary Fiber	4 grams	4 grams
Protein	6 grams	6 grams
Sodium	346 milligrams	339 milligrams

Exchanges

	2 starch	2 starch

BREAD MIX

ingredients: 13 cups bread flour
2 tbsp. salt
1/2 cup sugar
1/2 cup nonfat dry milk

directions: Combine all ingredients in a large bowl. Stir together and distribute evenly. Store in large con-
tainer or divide into smaller containers (2 1/4 cups
for 1-pound loves; 3 1/3 cups for 1 1/2-pound
loaves) for up to 6 months.
Use bread mix in Simple Mix Bread* and Glazed
Cinnamon Raisin Bread*.

Nutrition per Serving (per cup of mix)

Calories	415
Carbohydrate	91 grams
Cholesterol	0 milligrams
Dietary Fiber	4 grams
Protein	13 grams
Sodium	937 milligrams

Susan Melton, South Carolina

BUTTERMILK BANANA BREAD

1-POUND RECIPE (8 SLICES)

ingredients:
1 tsp. yeast
1/2 tsp. salt
2 1/8 cups bread flour
1/2 cup mashed bananas
1/4 cup skim milk
1 tsp. lemon juice
1/2 cup water

1 1/2-POUND RECIPE (12 SLICES)

ingredients:
1 1/2 tsp. yeast
3/4 tsp. salt
3 cups + 3 tbsp. bread flour
2/3 cup mashed bananas
1/3 cup skim milk
1 1/2 tsp. lemon juice
2/3 cup water

directions: Add ingredients in the order suggested by the bread machine manufacturer and follow baking instructions provided in the manual.

Nutrition per Serving	1-Pound	1 1/2-Pound
Calories	118	117
Carbohydrate	26 grams	23 grams
Cholesterol	< 1 milligram	< 1 milligram
Dietary Fiber	2 grams	2 grams
Protein	4 grams	4 grams
Sodium	140 milligrams	139 milligrams

Exchanges

	1 1/2 starch	1 1/2 starch

BUTTERMILK BREAD

1-POUND RECIPE (8 SLICES)

ingredients:
1 tsp. yeast
1/4 tsp. baking soda
1/2 tsp. salt
2 1/2 cups bread flour
2 tbsp. honey
2 tbsp. lite applesauce
1 tbsp. lemon juice
1 cup skim milk

1 1/2-POUND RECIPE (12 SLICES)

ingredients:
1 1/2 tsp. yeast
1/4 tsp. baking soda
3/4 tsp. salt
3 1/4 cups bread flour
3 tbsp. honey
3 tbsp. lite applesauce
1 1/4 tbsp. lemon juice
1 1/4 cup skim milk

directions:
Combine milk with lemon juice and let stand 10 minutes. Add ingredients in the order suggested by the bread machine manufacturer and follow baking instructions provided in the manual.

Nutrition per Serving	1-Pound	1 1/2-Pound
Calories	157	138
Carbohydrate	32 grams	28 grams
Cholesterol	< 1 milligram	< 1 milligram
Dietary Fiber	2 grams	2 grams
Protein	6 grams	5 grams
Sodium	178 milligrams	166 milligrams

Exchanges

	2 starch	1 3/4 starch

CAPPUCCINO YOGURT BREAD

1-POUND RECIPE (8 SLICES)

ingredients:
1 1/2 tsp. yeast
1/2 tsp. salt
1 tbsp. applesauce
1 tbsp. sugar
2 1/3 cups bread flour
3 1/4 cups water
1/2 cup fat-free cappuccino yogurt

1 1/2-POUND RECIPE (12 SLICES)

ingredients:
2 1/2 tsp. yeast
1 1/4 tsp. salt
2 tbsp. applesauce
2 tbsp. sugar
3 1/2 cups bread flour
3/4 cup water
3/4 cup fat-free cappuccino yogurt

directions: Add ingredients in the order suggested by the bread machine manufacturer and follow baking instructions provided in the manual.

Nutrition per Serving	1-Pound	1 1/2-Pound
Calories	131	128
Carbohydrate	25 grams	25 grams
Cholesterol	< 1 milligram	< 1 milligram
Dietary Fiber	2 grams	2 grams
Protein	5 grams	5 grams
Sodium	214 milligrams	237 milligrams

CARROT-PUMPKIN BREAD

1-POUND RECIPE (8 SLICES)

ingredients:
1 1/2 tsp. yeast
3/4 tsp. salt
1/2 tsp. cinnamon
2 cups bread flour
1/3 cup canned carrot slices, mashed
1/3 cup canned pumpkin, mashed
1/3 cup lite applesauce
1 tbsp. apple butter
1 tbsp. honey
1/4 cup water

1 1/2-POUND RECIPE (12 SLICES)

ingredients:
2 tsp. yeast
1 tsp. salt
3/4 tsp. cinnamon
3 cups bread flour
1/2 cup canned carrot slices, mashed
1/2 cup canned pumpkin, mashed
1/2 cup lite applesauce
1 1/2 tbsp. apple butter
2 tbsp. honey
1/3 cup water

directions:
Add ingredients in the order suggested by the bread machine manufacturer and follow baking instructions provided in the manual.

Nutrition per Serving	1-Pound	1 1/2-Pound
Calories	129	127
Carbohydrate	27 grams	26 grams
Cholesterol	0 milligrams	0 milligrams
Dietary Fiber	2 grams	2 grams
Protein	4 grams	4 grams
Sodium	183 milligrams	205 milligrams

Exchanges

	1 1/3 starch	1 1/3 starch
	1/2 fruit	1/2 fruit

CARROT-RAISIN BREAD

1-POUND RECIPE (8 SLICES)

ingredients:
1 1/2 tsp. yeast
1/4 tsp. salt
1 1/2 tsp. cinnamon
2 tbsp. nonfat dry milk powder
1 3/4 cup bread flour
1/2 cup whole wheat flour
1/4 cup mashed banana
1/2 cup shredded carrots
1/2 cup water
1/2 cup raisins

1 1/2-POUND RECIPE (12 SLICES)

ingredients:
2 tsp. yeast
1/2 tsp. salt
2 tsp. cinnamon
3 tbsp. nonfat dry milk powder
2 1/4 cups bread flour
1 cup whole wheat flour
1/3 cup mashed bananas
3/4 cup shredded carrots
3/4 cup water
3/4 cup raisins

directions: Add ingredients in the order suggested by the bread machine manufacturer and follow baking instructions provided in the manual.

Nutrition per Serving	1-Pound	1 1/2-Pound
Calories	155	150
Carbohydrate	33 grams	32 grams
Cholesterol	< 1 milligram	< 1 milligram
Dietary Fiber	3 grams	3 grams
Protein	5 grams	5 grams
Sodium	78 milligrams	101 milligrams

Exchanges

	1-Pound	1 1/2-Pound
	1 2/3 starch	1 2/3 starch
	1/2 fruit	1/2 fruit

CHEESE BREAD

instructions:

1-POUND RECIPE (8 SLICES)
1 1/2 tsp. yeast
1/2 tsp. salt
1 1/2 tsp. sugar
2 cups bread flour
1/2 cup nonfat shredded Cheddar cheese
1/2 cup egg substitute
2 tbsp. lite applesauce
1/3 cup flat beer*

ingredients:

1 1/2-POUND RECIPE (12 SLICES)
2 tsp. yeast
3/4 tsp. salt
2 tsp. sugar
3 cups bread flour
1 cup nonfat shredded Cheddar cheese
1/2 cup egg substitute
1 egg white
1/4 cup lite applesauce
1/2 cup flat beer*

directions:
*Pour beer into bowl and leave at room temperature for 1 to 2 hours, until beer becomes flat. Add ingredients in the order suggested by the bread machine manufacturer and follow baking instructions provided in the manual.

Nutrition per Serving	1-Pound	1 1/2-Pound
Calories	130	133
Carbohydrate	23 grams	23 grams
Cholesterol	0 milligrams	0 milligrams
Dietary Fiber	2 grams	2 grams
Protein	7 grams	8 grams
Sodium	226 milligrams	248 milligrams

Exchanges

	1 1/2 starch	1 1/2 starch
	1/2 meat	2 meat

CHERRY BANANA VANILLA YOGURT BREAD

1-POUND RECIPE (8 SLICES)

ingredients:
1 tsp. yeast
3/4 tsp. salt
1 tbsp. nonfat dry milk powder
2 1/4 cups bread flour
1 tbsp. sugar
1 tbsp. lite applesauce
1/2 cup nonfat cherry-vanilla yogurt
1/2 cup water
1/2 banana

1 1/2-POUND RECIPE (12 SLICES)

ingredients:
1 1/2 tsp. yeast
1 1/4 tsp. salt
2 tbsp. nonfat dry milk powder
3 1/4 cups bread flour
2 tbsp. sugar
2 tbsp. lite applesauce
3/4 cup nonfat cherry-vanilla yogurt
3/4 cup water
3/4 banana

directions:
Add ingredients in the order suggested by the bread machine manufacturer and follow baking instructions provided in the manual.

Nutrition per Serving	1-Pound	1 1/2-Pound
Calories	131	128
Carbohydrate	26 grams	25 grams
Cholesterol	< 1 milligram	< 1 milligram
Dietary Fiber	2 grams	2 grams
Protein	5 grams	5 grams
Sodium	214 milligrams	214 milligrams
Exchanges	1 2/3 starch	1 2/3 starch

CHOCOLATE BREAD

ingredients: **1-POUND RECIPE (8 SLICES)**
1 1/2 tsp. yeast
1/2 tsp. salt
3/4 tsp. cinnamon
1/4 cup sugar
2 tbsp. unsweetened cocoa powder
2 1/3 cups bread flour
2/3 cup skim milk
1/4 cup egg substitute
3 tbsp. apple butter

ingredients: **1 1/2-POUND RECIPE (12 SLICES)**
2 1/2 tsp. yeast
3/4 tsp. salt
1 tsp. cinnamon
1/3 cup sugar
3 tbsp. unsweetened cocoa powder
3 cups bread flour
3/4 cup skim milk
1/3 cup egg substitute
1/4 cup apple butter

directions: Add ingredients in the order suggested by the bread machine manufacturer and follow baking instructions provided in the manual.

Nutrition per Serving	1-Pound	1 1/2-Pound
Calories	171	148
Carbohydrate	35 grams	31 grams
Cholesterol	< 1 milligram	< 1 milligram
Dietary Fiber	2 grams	2 grams
Protein	6 grams	5 grams
Sodium	158 milligrams	155 milligrams

Exchanges

	1-Pound	1 1/2-Pound
	2 starch	1 3/4 starch
	1/3 fruit	1/3 fruit

* For you chocoholics you may add 3 tablespoons chocolate syrup in 1 pound and 4 tablespoons in 1 1/2 pound. Absolutely delicious! Calories and exchanges are not included with this extra. Still Fat-Free!

CINNAMON-APPLE-RAISIN BREAD

1-POUND RECIPE (8 SLICES)

ingredients:
1 1/2 tsp. yeast
1/4 tsp. salt
1/3 cup multi-grain oatmeal
1 cup whole wheat flour
1 1/2 cups bread flour
3/4 tsp. cinnamon
1/2 cup apple butter
3/4 cup water
2 tbsp. raisins

1 1/2-POUND RECIPE (12 SLICES)

ingredients:
2 1/4 tsp. yeast
1/2 tsp. salt
1/2 cup multi-grain oatmeal
1 1/3 cups whole wheat flour
2 cups bread flour
1 tsp. cinnamon
3/4 cup apple butter
1 cup water
1/3 cup raisins

directions: Add ingredients in the order suggested by the bread machine manufacturer and follow baking instructions provided in the manual.

Nutrition per Serving	1-Pound	1 1/2-Pound
Calories	185	176
Carbohydrate	40 grams	38 grams
Cholesterol	0 milligrams	0 milligrams
Dietary Fiber	4 grams	3 grams
Protein	6 grams	5 grams
Sodium	70 milligrams	92 milligrams

Exchanges

	1-Pound	1 1/2-Pound
	2 starch	1 2/3 starch
	2/3 fruit	2/3 fruit

CINNAMON BUBBLE LOAF

1-POUND RECIPE

ingredients: 1-pound Sweet Dough Recips (see page 109)
2 tbsp. fat-free margarine, melted
2/3 cup brown sugar
1 tsp. cinnamon

1 1/2-POUND RECIPE

ingredients: 1 1/2-pound Sweet Dough Recipe
3 tbsp. fat-free margarine, melted
3/4 cup brown sugar
1 1/2 tsp. cinnamon

directions: Prepare Sweet Dough according to directions. Turn dough onto lightly floured surface and roll into long rope. Lightly spray 9x5-inch loaf pan (1 1/2-pound recipe) or 8x4-inch loaf pan (1-pound recipe) with nonfat cooking spray. Divide dough into 40 to 60 pieces and roll each piece into a small ball. In a small bowl, combine sugar and cinnamon; mix well. Dip each dough ball into melted margarine; roll in cinnamon-sugar mixture. Layer dough balls in prepared pan; sprinkle remaining cinnamon-sugar mixture over top of dough. Cover dough and let rise in warm place 30 to 45 minutes, until doubled in size. Preheat oven to 350 degrees. Bake in preheated oven 25 to 30 minutes, until lightly browned. Invert rolls onto large serving platter and serve immediately.

Nutrition per Serving	1-Pound	1 1/2-Pound
Calories	154	161
Carbohydrate	34 grams	35 grams
Cholesterol	< 1 milligram	< 1 milligram
Dietary Fiber	1 gram	1 gram
Protein	4 grams	4 grams
Sodium	141 milligrams	157 milligrams

Exchanges

	1 1/3 starch	1 1/3 starch
	3/4 fruit	1 fruit

CINNAMON-PEACH BREAD

1-POUND RECIPE (8 SLICES)

ingredients:
1 1/2 tsp. yeast
3/4 tsp. salt
1/4 tsp. cinnamon
1/4 tsp. nutmeg
2 cups bread flour
1 tbsp. nonfat dry milk
2 tsp. brown sugar
1/3 cup nonfat vanilla yogurt
2 tbsp. cinnamon applesauce
1/2 cup water
1/2 cup dried peaches

1 1/2-POUND RECIPE (12 SLICES)

ingredients:
2 tsp. yeast
1 tsp. salt
1/2 tsp. cinnamon
1/2 tsp. nutmeg
3 cups bread flour
1 1/2 tbsp. nonfat dry milk
1 tbsp. brown sugar
1/2 cup nonfat vanilla yogurt
1/4 cup cinnamon applesauce
3/4 cup water
3/4 cup dried peaches

directions:
Add ingredients in the order suggested by the bread machine manufacturer and follow baking instructions provided in the manual.

Nutrition per Serving	1-Pound	1 1/2-Pound
Calories	142	142
Carbohydrate	29 grams	29 grams
Cholesterol	< 1 milligram	< 1 milligram
Dietary Fiber	2 grams	2 grams
Protein	5 grams	5 grams
Sodium	191 milligrams	214 milligrams

Exchanges

	1 2/3 starch	1 2/3 starch

CINNAMON-RAISIN BREAD

1-POUND RECIPE (8 SLICES)

ingredients:
1 1/2 tsp. yeast
3/4 tsp. salt
1 tsp. cinnamon
3 cups bread flour
3 tbsp. honey
3 tbsp. lite applesauce
1/2 cup egg substitute
3/4 cup skim milk
1/3 cup raisins

1 1/2-POUND RECIPE (12 SLICES)

ingredients:
2 1/2 tsp. yeast
1 tsp. salt
1 3/4 tsp. cinnamon
3 1/2 cups bread flour
1/4 cup honey
1/4 cup lite applesauce
1/2 cup egg substitute
1 egg white
1 cup skim milk
1/2 cup raisins

directions: Add ingredients in the order suggested by the bread machine manufacturer and follow baking instructions provided in the manual.

Nutrition per Serving	1-Pound	1 1/2-Pound
Calories	214	173
Carbohydrate	44 grams	36 grams
Cholesterol	< 1 milligram	< 1 milligram
Dietary Fiber	2 grams	2 grams
Protein	8 grams	6 grams
Sodium	237 milligrams	205 milligrams

Exchanges

	1-Pound	1 1/2-Pound
	2 2/3 starch	2 starch
	1/3 fruit	1/3 fruit

CINNAMON ROLLS

1-POUND RECIPE (10 ROLLS)

ingredients: 1-Pound recipe Sweet Dough (see page 109)
1 1/2 tbsp. fat-free margarine, melted
1/4 cup sugar
1 1/2 tsp. cinnamon
1/2 cup powdered sugar
1 1/2 tsp. skim milk
1/4 tsp. vanilla

1 1/2-POUND RECIPE (16 ROLLS)

ingredients: 1 1/2-Pound recipe Sweet Dough
2 tbsp. fat-free margarine, melted
1/3 cup sugar
2 tsp. cinnamon
1 cup powdered sugar
2 1/2 tsp. skim milk
1/2 tsp. vanilla

directions: Prepare Sweet Bread Dough according to directions. Turn dough onto lightly floured surface; shape into log. Lightly spray two 9-inch cake pans (1 1/2-pound recipe) or one 9-inch cake pan (1-pound recipe) with nonfat cooking spray. Roll dough into rectangle until dough is even and smooth. In small bowl, combine sugar and cinnamon; mix well. Brush dough with melted margarine; sprinkle with cinnamon-sugar mixture. Roll dough up lengthwise; seal ends. Cut into equal pieces; place in prepared pans. Cover; let rise in warm place 30 to 45 minutes, until doubled in size. Preheat oven to 350 degrees. Bake rolls in preheated oven 20 to 25 minutes, until lightly browned. Cool rolls 10 to 15 minutes.

In small bowl, combine powdered sugar, milk, and vanilla and mix until smooth, thin consistency. Drizzle icing over rolls and serve. Cinnamon rolls can be reheated in microwave on high 15 seconds.

Nutrition per Serving	1-Pound	1 1/2-Pound
Calories	169	148
Carbohydrate	37 grams	32 grams
Cholesterol	< 1 milligram	< 1 milligram
Dietary Fiber	1 gram	1 gram
Protein	5 grams	4 grams
Sodium:	160 milligrams	149 milligrams
Exchanges	1 2/3 starch	1 1/3 starch
	3/4 fruit	3/4 fruit

CINNAMON STICKS

1-POUND RECIPE (8 STICKS)

ingredients: 1 1/2 tsp. yeast
1/2 tsp. salt
1/4 cup sugar, divided
2 3/4 cups bread flour
3/4 cup + 1 tbsp. water
3/4 tbsp. cinnamon

1 1/2-POUND RECIPE (12 STICKS)

ingredients: 2 tsp. yeast
3/4 tsp. salt
6 tbsp. sugar, divided
3 1/3 cups bread flour
1 cup + 3 tbsp. water
1 tbsp. cinnamon

directions: Add yeast, salt, 1 or 2 tablespoons sugar (1-pound or 1 1/2-pound recipe), bread flour, and water to bread machine in order suggested by bread machine manufacturer; process on dough cycle. Remove dough from machine; divide into 8 to 12 equal pieces. Roll each piece into 6-inch log. Lightly spray baking sheet with nonfat cooking spray. Place bagel sticks on baking sheet. Cover with plastic wrap; let rise until puffy, about 20 minutes. In small bowl, combine remaining sugar with cinnamon; mix well. Boil dough sticks in 3 to 4 inches of boiling water, 1 minute per side; drain on towel. Preheat oven to 400 degrees. Roll logs in cinnamon-sugar mixture to coat. Place on prepared pan; bake in preheated oven 20 to 25 minutes, until lightly browned.

Nutrition per Serving	1-Pound	1 1/2-Pound
Calories	139	166
Carbohydrate	29 grams	34 grams
Cholesterol	0 milligrams	0 milligrams
Dietary Fiber	2 grams	2 grams
Protein	4 grams	5 grams
Sodium	136 milligrams	137 milligrams
Exchanges	1 1/3 starch	1 2/3 starch
	1/2 fruit	1/2 fruit

CINNAMON-SUGAR MONKEY ROLLS

ingredients:

20 ROLLS
1 1/2 tsp. yeast
1/2 tsp. salt
1/3 cup + 2 tbsp. sugar
1 tsp. cinnamon
2 1/2 cups bread flour
1 tbsp. low-fat margarine
2 tbsp. fat-free margarine, melted
1/4 cup egg substitute
1/2 cup skim milk
2 tbsp. water

directions:

Add yeast, salt, 2 tablespoons sugar, flour, low-fat margarine, water, egg substitute, and milk in the order suggested by bread machine manufacturer; process on dough cycle. When cycle is complete, remove dough from machine; place on lightly-floured surface. Divide dough into 20 equal pieces; form each piece into ball. In small bowl, combine 1/3 cup sugar with cinnamon; mix well. Roll each ball into melted margarine, coat with cinnamon-sugar mixture. Lightly spray 8-cup oven-proof ring mold or tube pan with nonfat cooking spray. Arrange half the coated balls in bottom of pan; repeat with second layer (place second layer between rolls on bottom). Drizzle dough with remaining melted margarine; sprinkle any remaining cinnamon-sugar on top. Cover pan; let rise in warm, draft-free place until almost doubled in size, about 45 minutes. Preheat oven to 375 degrees. Bake rolls 25 to 30 minutes, until golden brown. Remove from oven; cool on rack 1 to 5 minutes and invert onto serving plate.

Nutrition per Serving

Calories	73
Carbohydrate	15 grams
Cholesterol	< 1 milligram
Dietary Fiber	1 gram
Protein	2 grams
Sodium	76 milligrams

Exchanges

1 starch

CORNBREAD

1-POUND RECIPE (8 SLICES)

ingredients:
1 1/2 tsp. yeast
1/2 tsp. salt
2 cups flour
1 cup cornmeal
2 tbsp. lite applesauce
1/4 cup egg substitute
1/4 cup molasses
3/4 cup skim milk

1 1/2-POUND RECIPE (12 SLICES)

ingredients:
2 tsp. yeast
1 tsp. salt
3 cups flour
1 cup cornmeal
4 tbsp. lite applesauce
1/4 cup egg substitute
1 egg white
1/3 cup molasses
1 cup skim milk

directions: Add ingredients in the order suggested by the bread machine manufacturer and follow baking instructions provided in the manual.

Nutrition per Serving	1-Pound	1 1/2-Pound
Calories	205	181
Carbohydrate	42 grams	37 grams
Cholesterol	< 1 milligram	< 1 milligram
Dietary Fiber	2 grams	2 grams
Protein	7 grams	6 grams
Sodium	160 milligrams	204 milligrams

Exchanges

	1-Pound	1 1/2-Pound
	2 1/3 starch	2 starch
	1/2 fruit	1/2 fruit

CORN DOGS

ingredients: 1-Pound Cornbread Recipe (see page 36)
8 fat-free hot dogs

directions: Add cornbread recipe ingredients in the order suggested by the bread machine manufacturer and process on the dough cycle. Divide dough into 8 equal pieces; roll each piece into rectangle. Place hot dog in center of dough; seal dough around the hot dog.
Preheat oven to 350 degrees. Lightly spray baking sheets with nonfat cooking spray. Place corn dogs on prepared baking sheet and bake in preheated oven 20 to 25 minutes, until lightly browned. Rotate corn dogs halfway through cooking time.

Serves: 8

Nutrition per Serving
Calories	159
Carbohydrate	26 grams
Cholesterol	15 milligrams
Dietary Fiber	2 grams
Protein	10 grams
Sodium	490 milligrams

Exchanges
1 2/3 starch
2/3 meat

CORN KERNEL BREAD

ingredients:

1-POUND RECIPE (8 SLICES)
1 1/2 tsp. yeast
3/4 tsp. salt
1 cup cornmeal
2 cups bread flour
1/4 cup egg substitute
3 tbsp. honey
2 1/2 tbsp. lite applesauce
1 1/2 tbsp. fat-free margarine
1 cup skim milk
1/2 cup cooked corn kernels

ingredients:

1 1/2-POUND RECIPE (12 SLICES)
2 1/2 tsp. yeast
1 tsp. salt
1 1/2 cups cornmeal
2 1/2 cups bread flour
1/4 cup egg substitute
1 whole egg white
1/4 cup honey
3 tbsp. lite applesauce
2 tbsp. fat-free margarine
1 1/3 cups skim milk
2/3 cup cooked corn kernels

directions: Add ingredients in the order suggested by the bread machine manufacturer and following baking instructions provided in the manual. Add corn during raisin-bread cycle, or 5 minutes before kneading is finished.

Nutrition per Serving	1-Pound	1 1/2-Pound
Calories	203	182
Carbohydrate	45 grams	40 grams
Cholesterol	< 1 milligram	< 1 milligram
Dietary Fiber	2 grams	2 grams
Protein	7 grams	6 grams
Sodium	244 milligrams	219 milligrams

Exchanges		
	2 1/4 starch	2 starch
	1/2 fruit	1/2 fruit

CRACKED WHEAT BREAD

1-POUND RECIPE (8 SLICES)

ingredients:
1 1/2 tsp. yeast
1/2 tsp. salt
2 cups bread flour
1 tbsp. lite applesauce
1 tbsp. honey
1/2 cup skim milk
1/2 cup cracked wheat
1/2 cup boiling water

1 1/2-POUND RECIPE (12 SLICES)

ingredients:
2 1/2 tsp. yeast
3/4 tsp. salt
3 cups bread flour
2 tbsp. lite applesauce
2 tbsp. honey
2/3 cup skim milk
1 cup cracked wheat
1 cup boiling water

directions:
Soak cracked wheat in boiling water for at least 1 hour. Add remaining ingredients in the order suggested by the bread machine manufacturer and follow baking instructions provided in the manual.

Nutrition per Serving	1-Pound	1 1/2-Pound
Calories	132	139
Carbohydrate	26 grams	28 grams
Cholesterol	< 1 milligram	< 1 milligram
Dietary Fiber	2 grams	2 grams
Protein	5 grams	5 grams
Sodium	145 milligrams	144 milligrams

Exchanges

	1 2/3 starch	1 2/3 starch

CRANBERRY BREAD

1-POUND RECIPE (8 SLICES)

ingredients:
1 1/2 tsp. yeast
1/2 tsp. salt
1 tbsp. sugar
1 tbsp. nonfat dry milk
2 1/4 cups bread flour
1/4 cup cranberry juice
1 tbsp. lite applesauce
1/2 cup water
1/4 cup Craisins

1 1/2-POUND RECIPE (12 SLICES)

ingredients:
2 tsp. yeast
3/4 tsp. salt
2 tbsp. sugar
2 tbsp. nonfat dry milk
3 1/4 cups bread flour
1/2 cup cranberry juice
2 tbsp. lite applesauce
3/4 cup water
1/3 cup Craisins

directions: Add ingredients in the order suggested by the bread machine manufacturer and follow baking instructions provided in the manual.

Nutrition per Serving	1-Pound	1 1/2-Pound
Calories	129	129
Carbohydrate	28 grams	28 grams
Cholesterol	< 1 milligram	< 1 milligram
Dietary Fiber	2 grams	2 grams
Protein	4 grams	4 grams
Sodium	137 milligrams	137 milligrams

Exchanges

	1 1/3 starch	1 1/3 starch
	2/3 fruit	2/3 fruit

CRANBERRY-RAISIN-APPLE BREAD

1-POUND RECIPE (8 SLICES)

ingredients:
1 1/2 tsp. yeast
3/4 tsp. salt
1/2 tsp. sugar
1 tbsp. nonfat dry milk
2 1/2 cups bread flour
1 tsp. cinnamon
3 tbsp. lite applesauce
1 cup water
1/4 cup raisins
1/4 cup dried cranberries

1 1/2-POUND RECIPE (12 SLICES)

ingredients:
2 1/2 tsp. yeast
1 tsp. salt
1 tsp. sugar
2 tbsp. nonfat dry milk
3 1/3 cups bread flour
1 1/2 tsp. cinnamon
4 tbsp. lite applesauce
1 1/2 cups water
1/2 cup raisins
1/2 cup dried cranberries

directions: Add ingredients in the order suggested by the bread machine manufacturer and follow baking instructions provided in the manual.

Nutrition per Serving	1-Pound	1 1/2-Pound
Calories	150	143
Carbohydrate	31 grams	30 grams
Cholesterol	< 1 milligram	< 1 milligram
Dietary Fiber	2 grams	2 grams
Protein	5 grams	5 grams
Sodium	207 milligrams	185 milligrams

Exchanges

	1 2/3 starch	1 2/3 starch
	1/3 fruit	1/3 fruit

CRANBERRY WHEAT BREAD

1-POUND RECIPE (8 SLICES)

directions:
1 1/2 tsp. yeast
3/4 tsp. salt
1 cup bread flour
1 1/4 cups + 2 tbsp. whole wheat flour
3 1/3 tbsp. brown sugar
2 tbsp. sugar
1 1/2 tbsp. lite applesauce
2 tbsp. honey
1/2 cup water
1/2 cup cranberries

1 1/2-POUND RECIPE (12 SLICES)

ingredients:
2 tsp. yeast
1 tsp. salt
1 1/2 cups bread flour
2 cups flour, whole-grain wheat
1/4 cup brown sugar
1/4 cup sugar
2 tbsp. lite applesauce
3 tbsp. honey
3/4 cup water
3/4 cup cranberries

directions: Add ingredients in the order suggested by the bread machine manufacturer and follow baking instructions provided in the manual.

Nutrition per Serving	1-Pound	1 1/2-Pound
Calories	177	174
Carbohydrate	39 grams	39 grams
Cholesterol	0 milligrams	0 milligrams
Dietary Fiber	4 grams	3 grams
Protein	5 grams	5 grams
Sodium	204 milligrams	182 milligrams

Exchanges

	1 2/3 starch	1 2/3 starch
	1 fruit	1 fruit

CUMIN BREAD

1-POUND RECIPE (8 SLICES)

ingredients:
1 1/2 tsp. yeast
3/4 tsp. salt
1/4 tsp. baking soda
1/3 tsp. minced garlic
1 1/2 tbsp. cumin seeds
2 1/2 cups bread flour
2 tbsp. honey
1 cup nonfat cottage cheese
1/2 cup egg substitute

1 1/2-POUND RECIPE (12 SLICES)

ingredients:
2 1/2 tsp. yeast
1 tsp. salt
1/3 tsp. baking soda
1/2 tsp. minced garlic
2 tbsp. cumin seeds
3 1/3 cups bread flour
3 tbsp. honey
1 1/3 cups nonfat cottage cheese
2/3 cup egg substitute

directions: Add ingredients in the order suggested by the bread machine manufacturer and follow baking instructions provided in the manual.

Nutrition per Serving	1-Pound	1 1/2-Pound
Calories	161	143
Carbohydrate	33 grams	30 grams
Cholesterol	< 1 milligram	< 1 milligram
Dietary Fiber	2 grams	2 grams
Protein	7 grams	6 grams
Sodium	271 milligrams	233 milligrams

Exchanges

	2 starch	1 3/4 starch

DATE-BRAN BREAD

ingredients:

1-POUND RECIPE (8 SLICES)
1 tsp. yeast
2 tbsp. nonfat dry milk powder
2 tsp. instant coffee powder
1 cup bread flour
1/3 cup whole wheat flour
1/3 cup bran
2 tbsp. molasses
2 tbsp. lite applesauce
1 cup water
1/2 cup chopped dates

ingredients:

1 1/2-POUND RECIPE (12 SLICES)
1 1/2 tsp. yeast
1/4 cup nonfat dry milk powder
1 tbsp. instant coffee powder
2 cups bread flour
2/3 cup whole wheat flour
2/3 cup bran
3 tbsp. molasses
3 tbsp. lite applesauce
1 1/3 cups water
3/4 cup chopped dates

directions: Add ingredients in the order suggested by the bread machine manufacturer and follow baking instructions provided in the manual.

Nutrition per Serving	1-Pound	1 1/2-Pound
Calories	123	148
Carbohydrate	29 grams	34 grams
Cholesterol	< 1 milligram	< 1 milligram
Dietary Fiber	3 grams	3 grams
Protein	4 grams	5 grams
Sodium	11 milligrams	13 milligrams

Exchanges

	1-Pound	1 1/2-Pound
	1 1/3 starch	1 2/3 starch
	1/2 fruit	1/3 fruit

DILL BREAD

1-POUND RECIPE (8 SLICES)

ingredients:
1 tsp. yeast
1/2 tsp. salt
2 tbsp. sugar
1/2 tsp. baking soda
3/4 tbsp. parsley flakes
1 1/2 tbsp. dill
2 cups bread flour
2 tbsp. minced dry onion flakes
3/4 cup nonfat cottage cheese
1/4 cup egg substitute
2 tbsp. water

1 1/2-POUND RECIPE (12 SLICES)

ingredients:
1 1/2 tsp. yeast
1 tsp. salt
2 1/2 tbsp. sugar
1/2 tsp. baking soda
1 tbsp. parsley flakes
2 tbsp. dill
3 cups flour
2 tbsp. minced dry onion flakes
1 cup nonfat cottage cheese
1/2 cup egg substitute
3 tbsp. water

directions: Add ingredients in the order suggested by the bread machine manufacturer and follow baking instructions provided in the manual.

Nutrition per Serving	1-Pound	1 1/2-Pound
Calories	127	124
Carbohydrate	27 grams	26 grams
Cholesterol	< 1 milligram	< 1 milligram
Dietary Fiber	1 gram	1 gram
Protein	5 grams	5 grams
Sodium	214 milligrams	242 milligrams

Exchanges

	1 1/2 starch	1 1/2 starch

DINNER ROLLS

ingredients:

12 ROLLS
1 1/2 tsp. yeast
3/4 tsp. salt
2 tbsp. sugar
2 1/3 cups bread flour
1/2 cup egg substitute
2 tbsp. lite applesauce

directions: Add ingredients in the order suggested by the bread machine manufacturer and process on the dough cycle. When cycle is complete, remove dough from the machine and place on a lightly-floured surface. Divide dough into 12 pieces and shape into desired shapes. Cover and let rise in a warm, draft-free place until almost doubled in size, about 20 to 30 minutes. Preheat oven to 375 degrees. Bake rolls 12 to 15 minutes, until golden brown.

Nutrition per Serving	12 Rolls
Calories	93
Carbohydrate	18 grams
Cholesterol	0 milligrams
Dietary Fiber	1 gram
Protein	4 grams
Sodium	149 milligrams

Exchanges

1 starch

EGG BREAD #1

1-POUND RECIPE (8 SLICES)

ingredients: 1 tsp. yeast
1/2 tsp. salt
1 tbsp. sugar
1 tbsp. nonfat dry milk powder
2 3/4 cups bread flour
1/3 cup egg substitute
1 cup skim milk

1 1/2-POUND RECIPE (12 SLICES)

ingredients: 1 1/2 tsp. yeast
3/4 tsp. salt
2 tbsp. sugar
2 tbsp. nonfat dry milk powder
3 1/4 cups bread flour
1/2 cup egg substitute
1 1/3 cups skim milk

directions: Add ingredients in the order suggested by the bread machine manufacturer and follow baking instructions provided in the manual.

Nutrition per Serving	1-Pound	1 1/2-Pound
Calories	163	135
Carbohydrate	31	26
Cholesterol	<1 milligram	<1 milligram
Dietary Fiber	2 grams	1 gram
Protein	7 grams	6 grams
Sodium	170 milligrams	167 milligrams

Exchanges

	2 starch	1 3/4 starch

EGG BREAD #2

ingredients: **1-POUND RECIPE (8 SLICES)**
1 1/2 tsp. yeast
3/4 tsp. salt
3 tbsp. sugar
2 cups bread flour
2 tbsp. lite applesauce
1/4 cup egg substitute
1/2 cup skim milk

ingredients: **1 1/2-POUND RECIPE (12 SLICES)**
2 1/2 tsp. yeast
1 tsp. salt
1/4 cup sugar
3 cups bread flour
3 tbsp. lite applesauce
1/2 cup egg substitute
3/4 cup skim milk

directions: Add ingredients in the order suggested by the bread machine manufacturer and follow baking instructions provided in the manual.

Nutrition per Serving	1-Pound	1 1/2-Pound
Calories	131	131
Carbohydrate	26 grams	26 grams
Cholesterol	<1 milligram	<1 milligram
Dietary Fiber	2 grams	2 grams
Protein	5 grams	5 grams
Sodium	220 milligrams	201 milligrams

Exchanges

	1 3/4 starch	1 3/4 starch

48

EVERYTHING-HEALTHY BREAD

1-POUND RECIPE (8 SLICES)

ingredients:
1 tsp. dry yeast
3/4 tsp. salt
1 1/2 cups bread flour
1/4 cup whole wheat flour
2 tsp. nonfat dry milk powder
1 tbsp. wheat germ
1/4 cup bran flakes
1 tbsp. lite applesauce
2 tsp. honey
3/4 cup water
1/4 cup grated carrots
2 tbsp. raisins
2 tbsp. chopped dates

1 1/2-POUND RECIPE (12 SLICES)

ingredients:
2 tsp. dry yeast
1 tsp. salt
2 cups bread flour
3/4 cup whole wheat flour
1 tbsp. nonfat dry milk powder
2 tbsp. wheat germ
1/2 cup bran flakes
2 tbsp. lite applesauce
1 tbsp. honey
1 1/4 cups water
1/2 cup grated carrots
1/4 cup raisins
1/4 cup chopped dates

directions: Add ingredients in the order suggested by the bread machine manufacturer and follow baking instructions provided in the manual.

Nutrition per Serving	1-Pound	1 1/2-Pound
Calories	122	136
Carbohydrate	26 grams	29 grams
Cholesterol	0 milligrams	0 milligrams
Dietary Fiber	2 grams	3 grams
Protein	4 grams	5 grams
Sodium	220 milligrams	203 milligrams
Exchanges	1 1/3 starch	1 2/3 starch
	1/3 fruit	1/3 fruit

FRENCH BREAD LOAF

ingredients:

1-POUND RECIPE (8 SLICES)
1 1/2 tsp. yeast
3/4 tsp. salt
1 tbsp. sugar
2 cups bread flour
3/4 cup water

ingredients:

1 1/2-POUND RECIPES (12 SLICES)
2 tsp. yeast
1 tsp. salt
1 1/2 tbsp. sugar
3 cups bread flour
1 cup water

directions: Add ingredients in the order suggested by the bread machine manufacturer and follow baking instructions provided in the manual. Set machine on dough cycle and process. Remove dough from machine, punch down, and roll into large ball. Place in medium-size bowl lightly sprayed with nonfat cooking spray. Cover bowl with towel or plastic wrap and let sit for 30 to 45 minutes, until doubled in bulk. Punch dough down and divide into 2 pieces. Roll each piece into 2 skinny loaves and place on baking sheet lightly sprayed with nonfat cooking spray. Using a very sharp knife, cut several slashes diagonally across the top of the baguettes. Cover the dough with towel or wrap and let it rise in a warm place until doubled in size, about 30 to 45 minutes.

Preheat oven to 350 degrees. Bake bread in preheated oven 15 to 20 minutes, until crust is lightly browned and loaves sound hollow when tapped.

Nutrition per Serving	1-Pound	1 1/2-Pound
Calories	110	109
Carbohydrate	22 grams	22 grams
Cholesterol	0 milligrams	0 milligrams
Dietary Fiber	2 grams	2 grams
Protein	4 grams	4 grams
Sodium	202 milligrams	180 milligrams
Exchanges	1 1/3 starch	1 1/3 starch

FRENCH SOURDOUGH BAGUETTES

1-POUND RECIPE (8 SLICES)

ingredients:
1 tsp. yeast
3/4 tsp. salt
1 tsp. sugar
2 cups bread flour
1/2 cup sourdough starter (see page 105)
2/3 cup water

1 1/2-POUND RECIPE (12 SLICES)

ingredients:
1 1/2 tsp. yeast
1 tsp. salt
2 tsp. sugar
3 cups bread flour
3/4 cup sourdough starter (see page 105)
3/4 cup water

directions:
Add ingredients in order suggested by the bread machine manufacturer and process on dough cycle. When cycle is complete, remove dough from machine and divide into 2 to 3 pieces. Roll each piece into long cylinder, tapering ends. Lightly spray baking sheet with nonfat cooking spray and place baguettes on sheet. Using a very sharp knife, slash 3 (14-inch-deep) diagonal cuts into the top of the baguettes. Cover bread with plastic wrap or a towel, and let rise in warm, draft-free place until doubled in size, about 30 to 45 minutes. Preheat oven to 450 degrees. Bake baguettes 12 to 15 minutes, until golden brown. Loaves should sound hollow when tapped.

Nutrition per Serving	1-Pound	1 1/2-Pound
Calories	109	110
Carbohydrate	22 grams	22 grams
Cholesterol	<1 milligram	<1 milligram
Dietary Fiber	1 gram	1 gram
Protein	4 grams	4 grams
Sodium	203 milligrams	181 milligrams
Exchanges	1 1/3 starch	1 1/3 starch

51

FRUIT AND SPICE BANANA BREAD

ingredients:
1-POUND RECIPE (8 SLICES)
1 1/4 tsp. yeast
1/4 tsp. salt
2 tbsp. nonfat dry milk powder
1 tsp. cinnamon
1/4 tsp. nutmeg
3/4 cup whole wheat flour
1 1/2 cups bread flour
1/2 cup mashed bananas
1/2 cup water
1/2 cup raisins

ingredients:
1 1/2-POUND RECIPE (12 SLICES)
1 3/4 tsp. yeast
1/2 tsp. salt
3 tbsp. nonfat dry milk powder
1 1/2 tsp. cinnamon
1/2 tsp. nutmeg
2/3 cup whole wheat flour
2 3/4 cups bread flour
3/4 cup mashed bananas
3/4 cup water
3/4 cup raisins

directions: Add ingredients in the order suggested by the bread machine manufacturer and follow baking instructions provided in the manual.

Nutrition per Serving	1-Pound	1 1/2-Pound
Calories	155	156
Carbohydrate	33 grams	33 grams
Cholesterol	<1 milligram	<1 milligram
Dietary Fiber	3 grams	3 grams
Protein	5 grams	5 grams
Sodium	176 milligrams	98 milligrams

Exchanges

	2 starch	2 starch

GLAZED CINNAMON RAISIN BREAD

1-POUND RECIPE (8 SLICES)

ingredients:
1 1/2 tsp. yeast
2 1/4 cups Bread Mix* (see page 20)
1 tsp. cinnamon
1 tbsp. lite applesauce
3/4 cup warm water
1/3 cup raisins
3/4 cup powdered sugar
1/4 tsp. vanilla
1-2 tbsp. skim milk

1 1/2-POUND RECIPE (12 SLICES)

ingredients:
2 tsp. yeast
3 1/3 cups Bread Mix* (see page 20)
1 1/2 tsp. cinnamon
1 1/2 tbsp. lite applesauce
1 1/4 cups warm water
1/2 c. raisins
1 cup powdered sugar
1/2 tsp. vanilla
1-2 tbsp. skim milk

directions:
Add yeast, bread mix, cinnamon, applesauce, water, and raisins in the order suggested by the bread machine manufacturer and follow baking instructions provided in the manual.

In a small bowl, combine powdered sugar and vanilla. Stir in enough skim milk to smooth consiste ncy for glaze. Drizzle over cooled bread.

Nutrition per Serving	1-Pound	1 1/2-Pound
Calories	176	170
Carbohydrate	38 grams	37 grams
Cholesterol	<1 milligram	<1 milligram
Dietary Fiber	2 grams	2 grams
Protein	5 grams	4 grams
Sodium	266 milligrams	268 milligrams
Exchanges	1 2/3 starch	1 1/3 starch
	2/3 fruit	1 fruit

Susan Melton, South Carolina

GRANOLA PUMPKIN BREAD

1-POUND RECIPE (8 SLICES)

ingredients:
1 1/2 tsp. yeast
1/2 tsp. salt
1/2 tsp. cinnamon
1/2 tsp. pumpkin pie spice
1/2 cup whole wheat flour
1 1/2 cups bread flour
1/4 cup egg substitute
1/2 cup canned pumpkin
1/4 cup skim milk
1 tbsp. Lighter Bake
1/3 cup nonfat granola

1 1/2-POUND RECIPE (12 SLICES)

ingredients:
2 tsp. yeast
3/4 tsp. salt
3/4 tsp. cinnamon
3/4 tsp. pumpkin pie spice
3/4 cup whole wheat flour
2 1/4 cups bread flour
1/4 cup egg substitute
1 egg white
3/4 cup canned pumpkin
1/3 cup skim milk
2 tbsp. Lighter Bake
1/2 cup nonfat granola

directions:
Add ingredients in the order suggested by the bread machine manufacturer and follow baking instructions provided in the manual.

Nutrition per Serving	1-Pound	1 1/2-Pound
Calories	141	145
Carbohydrate	29 grams	30 grams
Cholesterol	1 milligram	1 milligram
Dietary Fiber	2 grams	2 grams
Protein	5 grams	5 grams
Sodium	153 milligrams	154 milligrams
Exchanges	1 1/3 starch	1 1/3 starch
	1/2 fruit	1/2 fruit

GREAT GRANOLA BREAD

ingredients:

1-POUND RECIPE (8 SLICES)

1 tsp. yeast
1/2 tsp. salt
1 tbsp. nonfat dry milk powder
1/2 cup nonfat granola
2 cups bread flour
3/4 tsp. cinnamon
1 tbsp. brown sugar
1 tbsp. frozen apple juice concentrate, thawed
3/4 cup + 2 tbsp. water

ingredients:

1 1/2-POUND RECIPE (12 SLICES)

1 1/2 tsp. yeast
3/4 tsp. salt
2 tbsp. nonfat dry milk powder
3/4 cup nonfat granola
3 cups bread flour
1 tsp. cinnamon
2 tbsp. brown sugar
2 tbsp. frozen apple juice concentrate, thawed
1 1/4 cups water

directions: Add ingredients in the order suggested by the bread machine manufacturer and follow baking instructions provided in the manual.

Nutrition per Serving	1-Pound	1 1/2-Pound
Calories	133	137
Carbohydrate	27 grams	29 grams
Cholesterol	<1 milligram	<1 milligram
Dietary Fiber	1 gram	1 gram
Protein	4 grams	4 grams
Sodium	140 milligrams	142 milligrams

Exchanges

	1 1/3 starch	1 1/3 starch
	1/2 fruit	1/2 fruit

HEALTHY LENTIL BREAD

ingredients:	**1-POUND RECIPE (8 SLICES)**
	1 1/4 tsp. yeast
	1/4 tsp. salt
	1/2 tsp. ground pepper
	3/4 cup whole wheat flour
	1 1/2 cups bread flour
	1 tsp. thyme
	1/4 tsp. onion powder
	3/4 cup cooked lentils
	2/3 cup water
ingredients:	**1 1/2-POUND RECIPE (12 SLICES)**
	2 tsp. yeast
	1/2 tsp. salt
	3/4 tsp. ground pepper
	2/3 cup whole wheat flour
	2 3/4 cups bread flour
	1 1/2 tsp. thyme
	1/2 tsp. onion powder
	1 1/8 cups cooked lentils
	1 cup water
directions:	Add ingredients in the order suggested by the bread machine manufacturer and follow baking instructions provided in the manual.

Nutrition per Serving	1-Pound	1 1/2-Pound
Calories	139	141
Carbohydrate	27 grams	28 grams
Cholesterol	0 milligrams	0 milligrams
Dietary Fiber	4 grams	3 grams
Protein	6 grams	6 grams
Sodium	69 milligrams	91 milligrams

Exchanges

	1-Pound	1 1/2-Pound
	1 3/4 starch	1 3/4 starch

HONEY-ALMOND BREAD

1-POUND RECIPE (8 SLICES)

ingredients:
1 tsp. yeast
3/4 tsp. salt
2 cups + 2 tbsp. bread flour
3/4 tsp. almond extract
2 tbsp. honey
1/4 cup egg substitute
2 tbsp. skim milk
1/2 cup water
2 tbsp. raisins
2 tbsp. Craisins
2 tbsp. dried mixed fruit

1 1/2-POUND RECIPE (12 SLICES)

ingredients:
1 1/2 tsp. yeast
1 tsp. salt
3 1/4 cups bread flour
1 tsp. almond extract
3 tbsp. honey
1/2 cup egg substitute
1/4 cup skim milk
3/4 cup water
1/4 cup raisins
1/4 cup Craisins
1/4 cup dried mixed fruit

directions:
Add ingredients in the order suggested by the bread manufacturer and follow baking instructions provided in the manual.

Nutrition per Serving	1-Pound	1 1/2-Pound
Calories	149	158
Carbohydrate	31 grams	33 grams
Cholesterol	<1 milligram	<1 milligram
Dietary Fiber	2 grams	2 grams
Protein	5 grams	5 grams
Sodium	215 milligrams	197 milligrams

Exchanges

	1 2/3 starch	1 2/3 starch
	1/3 fruit	1/2 fruit

HONEY-BANANA BREAD

1-POUND RECIPE (8 SLICES)

ingredients:
1 tsp. yeast
2 1/4 cups bread flour
1/4 cup nonfat dry milk powder
2 tbsp. brown sugar
1/4 cup egg substitute
1 tbsp. honey
1 tbsp. lite applesauce
5/8 cup water
1/2 banana

1 1/2-POUND RECIPE (12 SLICES)

ingredients:
1 1/2 tsp. yeast
3 1/4 cups bread flour
1/3 cup nonfat dry milk powder
3 tbsp. brown sugar
1/4 cup egg substitute
1 1/2 tbsp. honey
1 1/2 tbsp. lite applesauce
1 cup water
3/4 banana

directions:
Add ingredients in the order suggested by the bread machine manufacturer and follow baking instructions provided in the manual.

Nutrition per Serving	1-Pound	1 1/2-Pound
Calories	154	142
Carbohydrate	31 grams	29 grams
Cholesterol	<1 milligram	<1 milligram
Dietary Fiber	2 grams	2 grams
Protein	6 grams	5 grams
Sodium	26 milligrams	21 milligrams

Exchanges

	2 starch	2 starch

HONEY-CARROT BREAD

1-POUND RECIPE (8 SLICES)

ingredients:
1 tsp. active dry yeast
3/4 tsp. salt
2 tsp. nonfat dry milk powder
2 cups bread flour
2 tbsp. nonfat sour cream
2 tbsp. honey
2/3 cup grated carrots
1/2 cup water

1 1/2-POUND RECIPE (12 SLICES)

ingredients:
1 1/2 tsp. active dry yeast
1 tsp. salt
1 tbsp. nonfat dry milk powder
3 1/4 cups bread flour
1/4 cup nonfat sour cream
1/4 cup honey
1 cup grated carrots
3/4 cup water

directions:
Add ingredients in the order suggested by the bread manufacturer and follow baking instructions provided in the manual.

Exchange per Serving	1-Pound	1 1/2-Pound
Calories	127	141
Carbohydrate	26 grams	29 grams
Cholesterol	0 milligrams	0 milligrams
Dietary Fiber	2 grams	2 grams
Protein	4 grams	5 grams
Sodium	210 milligrams	189 milligrams

Exchanges

	1 1/3 starch	1 2/3 starch
	1/3 fruit	1/3 fruit

HONEY-DATE BREAD

1-POUND RECIPE (8 SLICES)

ingredients: 1 1/2 tsp. yeast
1/2 tsp. salt
2 cups bread flour
1/2 tbsp. lite applesauce
1 1/2 tbsp. honey
3/8 cup skim milk, warmed
3/8 cup + 1 tbsp. water
1/2 cup chopped dates

1 1/2-POUND RECIPE (12 SLICES)

ingredients: 2 tsp. yeast
3/4 tsp. salt
3 cups bread flour
1 tbsp. lite applesauce
2 tbsp. honey
1/2 cup skim milk, warmed
5/8 cup water
3/4 cup chopped dates

directions: Add ingredients in the order suggested by the bread manufacturer and follow baking instructions provided in the manual.

Nutrition per Serving	1-Pound	1 1/2-Pound
Calories	151	149
Carbohydrate	32 grams	32 grams
Cholesterol	<1 milligram	<1 milligram
Dietary Fiber	3 grams	2 grams
Protein	5 grams	4 grams
Sodium	142 milligrams	141 milligrams

Exchanges

	1-Pound	1 1/2-Pound
	1 1/3 starch	1 1/3 starch
	2/3 fruit	2/3 fruit

HONEY-LEMON BREAD

1-POUND RECIPE (8 SLICES)

ingredients:
1 1/2 tsp. yeast
1/2 tsp. salt
2 1/2 cups bread flour
1 1/2 tbsp. lemon zest, grated
1/4 cup honey
1/4 cup egg substitute
1 1/2 tbsp. apple butter
1 cup nonfat cottage cheese
1/4 cup water

1 1/2-POUND RECIPE (12 SLICES)

ingredients:
2 1/2 tsp. yeast
3/4 tsp. salt
3 cups bread flour
2 tbsp. lemon zest, grated
1/3 cup honey
1/3 cup egg substitute
2 tbsp. apple butter
1 1/4 cups nonfat cottage cheese
1/3 cup water

directions:
Add ingredients in the order suggested by the bread machine manufacturer and follow baking instructions provided in the manual.

Nutrition per Serving	1-Pound	1 1/2-Pound
Calories	177	147
Carbohydrate	36 grams	30
Cholesterol	<1 milligram	<1 milligram
Dietary Fiber	2 grams	2 grams
Protein	6 grams	5 grams
Sodium	170 milligrams	165 milligrams

Exchanges

	2 starch	1 2/3 starch
	1/3 fruit	1/3 fruit

HONEY WHEAT BREAD

1-POUND RECIPE (8 SLICES)

ingredients: 1 tsp. yeast
1 tsp. salt
1 tbsp. nonfat dry milk powder
2 1/4 cups whole wheat flour
1 tbsp. apple butter
2 tsp. honey
1 cup + 1 tbsp. water

1 1/2-POUND RECIPE (12 SLICES)

ingredients: 1 1/2 tsp. yeast
1 1/2 tsp. salt
3 1/4 cups whole wheat flour
2 tbsp. nonfat dry milk powder
2 tbsp. apple butter
1 tbsp. honey
1 1/4 cups + 3 tbsp. water

directions: Add ingredients in the order suggested by the bread machine manufactuer and follow baking instructions provided in the manual.

Nutrition per Serving	1-Pound	1 1/2-Pound
Calories	129	127
Carbohydrate	28 grams	27 grams
Cholesterol	<1 milligram	<1 milligram
Dietary Fiber	5 grams	4 grams
Protein	5 grams	5 grams
Sodium	271 milligrams	272 milligrams

Exchanges

	1 2/3 starch	1 2/3 starch

ITALIAN CHEESE BREAD

1-POUND RECIPE (8 SLICES)

ingredients:
1 tsp. yeast
1/2 tsp. salt
1 tsp. Italian seasoning
1 tbsp. sugar
1 tbsp. nonfat dry milk powder
1/4 cup nonfat Parmesan cheese
2 cups bread flour
3/4 cup water
1 tbsp. skim milk

1 1/2-POUND RECIPE (12 SLICES)

ingredients:
2 tsp. yeast
1 tsp. salt
2 tsp. Italian seasoning
2 tbsp. sugar
2 tbsp. nonfat dry milk powder
1/3 cup nonfat Parmesan cheese
3 cups bread flour
1 cup water
2 tbsp. skim milk

directions:
Add ingredients in the order suggested by the bread machine manufacturer and follow baking instructions provided in the manual.

Nutrition per Serving	1-Pound	1 1/2-Pound
Calories	118	121
Carbohydrate	23 grams	24 grams
Cholesterol	<1 milligram	<1 milligram
Dietary Fiber	1 gram	1 gram
Protein	5 grams	5 grams
Sodium	162 milligrams	205 milligrams

Exchanges

	1 1/2 starch	1 1/2 starch

LEMON-ORANGE BREAD

1-POUND RECIPE (8 SLICES)

ingredients: 1 tsp. active dry yeast
3/4 tsp. salt
2 tsp. sugar
1 tbsp. nonfat dry milk
2 cups bread flour
1 tbsp. apple butter
2 tbsp. orange marmalade
1 tbsp. lemon juice
2/3 cup water

1 1/2-POUND RECIPE (12 SLICES)

ingredients: 1 1/2 tsp. active dry yeast
1 tsp. salt
1 tbsp. sugar
2 tbsp. nonfat dry milk
3 cups bread flour
2 tbsp. apple butter
1/4 cup orange marmalade
2 tbsp. lemon juice
1 cup water

directions: Add ingredients in the order suggested by the bread machine manufacturer and follow baking instructions provided in the manual.

Nutrition per Serving	1-Pound	1 1/2-Pound
Calories	127	134
Carbohydrate	26 grams	28 grams
Cholesterol	<1 milligram	<1 milligram
Dietary Fiber	1 gram	1 gram
Protein	4 grams	4 grams
Sodium	206 milligrams	185 milligrams

Exchanges

	1 1/3 starch	1 1/3 starch
	1/2 fruit	1/3 fruit

MOLASSES-RAISIN BREAD

1-POUND RECIPE (8 SLICES)

ingredients:
1 1/2 tsp. yeast
3/4 tsp. salt
2 cups bread flour
1/2 cup whole wheat flour
3/4 cup multi-grain oatmeal
1 tbsp. instant espresso powder
1/3 cup molasses
3 tbsp. Lighter Bake
3/4 cup skim milk
1/2 cup raisins

1 1/2-POUND RECIPE (12 SLICES)

ingredients:
2 1/2 tsp. yeast
1 tsp. salt
2 1/4 cups bread flour
3/4 cup whole wheat flour
1 cup multi-grain oatmeal
1 1/2 tbsp. instant espresso powder
1/2 cup molasses
1/4 cup Lighter Bake
1 cup skim milk
3/4 cup raisins

directions:
Add ingredients in the order suggested by the bread machine manufacturer and follow baking instructions provided in the manual.

Nutrition per Serving	1-Pound	1 1/2-Pound
Calories	232	202
Carbohydrate	52 grams	46 grams
Cholesterol	<1 milligram	<1 milligram
Dietary Fiber	4 grams	3 grams
Protein	7 grams	6 grams
Sodium	229 milligrams	205 milligrams

Exchanges

	2 1/3 starch	2 starch
	1 fruit	1 fruit

MOLASSES WHOLE WHEAT BREAD

1-POUND RECIPE (8 SLICES)

ingredients:
1 tsp. yeast
3/4 tsp. salt
2 1/2 cups whole wheat flour
1 tbsp. nonfat dry milk powder
1 tbsp. apple butter
2 tbsp. molasses
1 cup water

1 1/2-POUND RECIPE (12 SLICES)

ingredients:
1 1/2 tsp. yeast
1 tsp. salt
3 1/4 cups whole wheat flour
1 1/2 tbsp. nonfat dry milk powder
1 1/2 tbsp. apple butter
3 tbsp. molasses
1 1/2 cups water

directions: Add ingredients in the order suggested by the bread machine manufacturer and follow baking instructions provided in the manual.

Nutrition per Serving	1-Pound	1 1/2-Pound
Calories	147	127
Carbohydrate	32 grams	27 grams
Cholesterol	<1 milligram	<1 milligram
Dietary Fiber	5 grams	4 grams
Protein	6 grams	4 grams
Sodium	209 milligrams	185 milligrams

Exchanges

	2 starch	1 2/3 starch

MUSTARD BREAD

1-POUND RECIPE (8 SLICES)

ingredients: 1 1/4 tsp. yeast
1/4 tsp. salt
1/2 tsp. dry mustard
1 1/2 tbsp. dried minced onions
2 cups bread flour
1 tsp. fat-free margarine
1 tsp. low-fat margarine
1 tbsp. prepared mustard
1/4 cup water
1/2 cup flat beer*

1 1/2-POUND RECIPE (12 SLICES)

ingredients: 1 3/4 tsp. yeast
1/2 tsp. salt
1 tsp. dry mustard
2 tbsp. dried minced onions
3 cups bread flour
1/2 tbsp. fat-free margarine
1/2 tbsp. low-fat margarine
2 tbsp. prepared mustard
1/3 cup water
3/4 cup flat beer*

directions: *Pour beer into small bowl and let stand at room temperature for at least 1 hour so it becomes flat. Add ingredients in the order suggested by the bread machine manufacturer and follow baking instructions provided in the manual.

Nutrition per Serving	1-Pound	1 1/2-Pound
Calories	116	117
Carbohydrate	22 grams	22 grams
Cholesterol	0 milligrams	0 milligrams
Dietary Fiber	2 grams	1 gram
Protein	4 grams	4 grams
Sodium	110 milligrams	144 milligrams

Exchanges

	1 1/3 starch	1 1/3 starch

OAT BRAN BREAD

1-POUND RECIPE (8 SLICES)

ingredients:
1 tsp. yeast
3/4 tsp. salt
3/4 cup bread flour
1 1/2 cups whole wheat flour
1/4 cup oat bran
1 tbsp. nonfat dry milk powder
1 tbsp. molasses
1 tbsp. Lighter Bake
1 cup + 1 tbsp. water

1 1/2-POUND RECIPE (12 SLICES)

ingredients:
1 1/2 tsp. yeast
1 tsp. salt
1 cup bread flour
2 1/4 cups whole wheat flour
1/3 cup oat bran
2 tbsp. nonfat dry milk powder
2 tbsp. molasses
2 tbsp. Lighter Bake
1 1/2 cups water

directions: Add ingredients in the order suggested by the bread machine manufacturer and follow baking instructions provided in the manual.

Nutrition per Serving	1-Pound	1 1/2-Pound
Calories	136	135
Carbohydrate	29 grams	29 grams
Cholesterol	<1 milligram	<1 milligram
Dietary Fiber	4 grams	4 grams
Protein	5 grams	5 grams
Sodium	208 milligrams	233 milligrams

Exchanges

	1-Pound	1 1/2-Pound
	1 2/3 starch	1 2/3 starch

OATMEAL-CRAISIN-BANANA BREAD

ingredients:

1-POUND RECIPE (SERVES 8)
1 1/2 tsp. yeast
1 tsp. salt
2 1/2 cups bread flour
2 tsp. nonfat dry milk powder
1 tsp. sugar
1/2 banana
1/4 cup craisins
1/4 cup oatmeal
1/2 tsp. cinnamon
1 cup water
3 tbsp. applesauce

ingredients:

1 1/2-POUND RECIPE (SERVES 12)
2 tsp. yeast
1 1/2 tsp. salt
3 1/2 cups bread flour
3 tbsp. nonfat dry milk powder
1 1/2 tsp. sugar
3/4 banana
1/2 cup crasins
1/2 cup oatmeal
1 tsp. oatmeal
1 tsp. cinnamon
1 1/2 cups water
4 tbsp. applesauce

directions: Add ingredients in the order suggested by the bread machine manufacturer and follow baking instructions provided in the manual.

Nutrition per Serving	1-Pound	1 1/2-Pound
Calories	166	164
Carbohydrate	34 grams	34 grams
Cholesterol	<1 milligram	<1 milligram
Dietary Fiber	2 grams	2 grams
Protein	6 grams	5 grams
Sodium	276 milligrams	275 milligrams

Exchanges	2 starch	2 starch

OATMEAL-MOLASSES BREAD

1-POUND RECIPE (8 SLICES)

ingredients:
1 1/2 tsp. yeast
3/4 tsp. salt
1 tbsp. brown sugar
2 cups bread flour
1/2 cup multi-grain oatmeal
2 tbsp. molasses
3/4 cup water

1 1/2-POUND RECIPE (12 SLICES)

ingredients:
1 1/2 tsp. yeast
1 tsp. salt
1 1/2 tbsp. brown sugar
3 cups bread flour
3/4 cup multi-grain oatmeal
3 tbsp. molasses
1 1/4 cups water

directions: Add ingredients in the order suggested by the bread machine manufacturer and follow baking instructions provided in the manual.

Nutrition per Serving	1-Pound	1 1/2-Pound
Calories	138	137
Carbohydrate	28 grams	28 grams
Cholesterol	0 milligrams	0 milligrams
Dietary Fiber	2 grams	2 grams
Protein	5 grams	4 grams
Sodium	209 milligrams	186 milligrams

Exchanges

	1 1/3 starch	1 1/3 starch
	2/3 fruit	2/3 fruit

ONION-CHEESE BREAD

1-POUND RECIPE (8 SLICES)

ingredients:
3/4 tsp. yeast
1/2 tsp. salt
1 1/2 tsp. dried minced onions
1 tbsp. sugar
2 tsp. nonfat dry milk powder
2 cups bread flour
1/4 cup nonfat shredded Cheddar cheese
1/4 cup nonfat shredded mozzarella cheese
2/3 cup water

1 1/2-POUND RECIPE (12 SLICES)

ingredients:
1 1/4 tsp. yeast
3/4 tsp. salt
2 tsp. dried minced onions
2 tbsp. sugar
1 tbsp. nonfat dry milk powder
3 cups bread flour
1/2 cup nonfat shredded Cheddar cheese
1/2 cup nonfat shredded mozzarella cheese
1 cup water

directions: Add ingredients in the order suggested by the bread machine manufacturer and follow baking instructions provided in the manual.

Nutrition per Serving	1-Pound	1 1/2-Pound
Calories	127	135
Carbohydrate	22 grams	23 grams
Cholesterol	<1 milligram	<1 milligram
Dietary Fiber	1 gram	1 gram
Protein	7 grams	8 grams
Sodium	223 milligrams	252 milligrams

Exchanges

	1 1/3 starch	1 1/3 starch
	1/2 meat	1/2 meat

ONION-POTATO BREAD

1-POUND RECIPE (8 SLICES)

ingredients: 1 3/4 tsp. yeast
3/4 tsp. salt
2 tsp. sugar
1/3 cup instant potato flakes
1 tbsp. freeze-dried chives
2 cups bread flour
3/4 cup water
1 tbsp. nonfat sour cream

1 1/2-POUND RECIPE (12 SLICES)

ingredients: 2 3/4 tsp. yeast
1 tsp. salt
1 tbsp. sugar
1/2 cup instant potato flakes
2 tbsp. freeze-dried chives
3 cups bread flour
1 cup + 2 tbsp. water
2 tbsp. nonfat sour cream

directions: Add ingredients in the order suggested by the bread machine manufacturer and follow baking instructions provided in the manual.

Nutrition per Serving	1-Pound	1 1/2-Pound
Calories	119	120
Carbohydrate	24 grams	24 grams
Cholesterol	6 milligrams	<1 milligram
Dietary Fiber	2 grams	2 grams
Protein	4 grams	4 grams
Sodium	204 milligrams	184 milligrams

Exchanges

	1 1/3 starch	1 1/3 starch

ONION-SEED BREAD

1-POUND RECIPE (8 SLICES)

ingredients:
1 1/2 tsp. yeast
3/4 tsp. salt
3/4 tsp. onion powder
3/4 tsp. minced onion flakes
3/4 tsp. poppy seeds
3/4 tsp. sesame seeds
2 cups bread flour
1 tbsp. lite applesauce
1 cup water

1 1/2-POUND RECIPE (12 SLICES)

ingredients:
2 1/2 tsp. yeast
1 tsp. salt
1 tsp. onion powder
1 tsp. minced onion flakes
1 tsp. poppy seeds
1 tsp. sesame seeds
3 cups bread flour
2 tbsp. lite applesauce
1 1/2 cups water

directions: Add ingredients in the order suggested by the bread machine manufacturer and follow baking instructions provided in the manual.

Nutrition per Serving	1-Pound	1 1/2-Pound
Calories	109	109
Carbohydrate	21 grams	21 grams
Cholesterol	0 milligrams	0 milligrams
Dietary Fiber	2 grams	2 grams
Protein	4 grams	4 grams
Sodium	203 milligrams	180 milligrams

Exchanges

	1 1/3 starch	1 1/3 starch

ORANGE BREAD

1-POUND RECIPE (8 SLICES)

ingredients: 1 1/2 tsp. yeast
3/4 tsp. salt
3 tbsp. nonfat dry milk powder
2 1/2 cups bread flour
3 tbsp. molasses
2 tbsp. apple butter
1 cup orange juice
2/3 cup navel orange, peeled and chopped

1 1/2-POUND RECIPE (12 SLICES)

ingredients: 2 1/2 tsp. yeast
1 tsp. salt
1/4 cup nonfat dry milk powder
3 1/4 cups bread flour
1/4 cup molasses
3 tbsp. apple butter
1 1/4 cups orange juice
3/4 cup navel orange, peeled and chopped

directions: Add ingredients in the order suggested by the bread machine manufacturer and follow baking instructions provided in the manual. Add the chopped oranges during the raisin-bread cycle, or 5 minutes before the kneading is finished.

Nutrition per Serving	1-Pound	1 1/2-Pound
Calories	182	167
Carbohydrate	38 grams	35 grams
Cholesterol	<1 milligram	<1 milligram
Dietary Fiber	2 grams	2 grams
Protein	6 grams	5 grams
Sodium	219 milligrams	195 milligrams

Exchanges

	1-Pound	1 1/2-Pound
	2 starch	1 2/3 starch
	1/2 fruit	2/3 fruit

ORANGE-CRANBERRY BREAD

1-POUND RECIPE (8 SLICES)

ingredients:
1 1/2 tsp. yeast
3/4 tsp. salt
2 cups bread flour
1 tbsp. apple butter
1 tsp. orange peel, grated
1/2 cup whole cranberry sauce
1/3 cup water

1 1/2-POUND RECIPE (12 SLICES)

ingredients:
2 tsp. yeast
1 tsp. salt
3 cups bread flour
2 tbsp. apple butter
2 tsp. orange peel
3/4 cup whole cranberry sauce
1/2 cup water

directions:
Add ingredients in the order suggested by the bread machine manufacturer and follow baking instructions provided in the manual.

Nutrition per Serving	1-Pound	1 1/2-Pound
Calories	135	136
Carbohydrate	28 grams	29 grams
Cholesterol	0 milligrams	0 milligrams
Dietary Fiber	2 grams	2 grams
Protein	4 grams	4 grams
Sodium	207 milligrams	185 milligrams

Exchanges

	1 3/4 starch	1 3/4 starch

ORANGE-HONEY WHEAT BREAD

1-POUND RECIPE (8 SLICES)

ingredients:
1 1/2 tsp. yeast
3/4 tsp. salt
1 tbsp. brown sugar
1 1/3 cups bread flour
2/3 cup whole wheat flour
1 tbsp. corn syrup
1 1/2 tbsp. Lighter Bake
3/4 cup water
1 tbsp. grated orange rind

1 1/2-POUND RECIPE (12 SLICES)

ingredients:
1 1/2 tsp. yeast
1 tsp. salt
2 tbsp. brown sugar
2 cups bread flour
1 cup whole wheat flour
2 tbsp. corn syrup
2 tbsp. Lighter Bake
1 cup water
1 1/2 tbsp. grated orange rind

directions: Add ingredients in the order suggested by the bread manufacturer and follow baking instructions provided in the manual.

Nutrition per Serving	1-Pound	1 1/2-Pound
Calories	125	128
Carbohydrate	26 grams	27 grams
Cholesterol	0 milligrams	0 milligrams
Dietary Fiber	2 grams	2 grams
Protein	4 grams	4 grams
Sodium	184 milligrams	205 milligrams

Exchanges		
	1 1/3 starch	1 1/3 starch
	1/3 fruit	1/3 fruit

ORANGE MARMALADE BREAD

1-POUND RECIPE (8 SLICES)

ingredients: 1 tsp. yeast
1/3 tsp. salt
1 1/3 cup bread flour
2/3 cup whole wheat flour
1 tbsp. apple butter
1/3 cup orange marmalade
2/3 cup water

1 1/2-POUND RECIPE (12 SLICES)

ingredients: 1 1/2 tsp. yeast
1/2 tsp. salt
2 1/2 cups bread flour
1/2 cup whole wheat flour
2 tbsp. apple butter
1/2 cup orange marmalade
1 cup water

directions: Add ingredients in the order suggested by the bread machine manufacturer and follow baking instructions provided in the manual.

Nutrition per Serving	1-Pound	1 1/2-Pound
Calories	144	146
Carbohydrate	31 grams	31 grams
Cholesterol	0 milligrams	0 milligrams
Dietary Fiber	2 grams	2 grams
Protein	4 grams	4 grams
Sodium	92 milligrams	92 milligrams

Exchanges

	1 1/3 starch	1 1/3 starch
	3/4 fruit	3/4 fruit

ORANGE WHEAT BREAD

1-POUND RECIPE (8 SLICES)

ingredients:
1 1/4 tsp. yeast
3/4 tsp. salt
1 tbsp. sugar
1 tbsp. nonfat dry milk powder
2 tbsp. wheat germ
3/4 cup whole wheat flour
1 1/4 cups bread flour
1 tbsp. apple butter
3/4 cup + 1 tbsp. water
1 tbsp. orange marmalade

1 1/2-POUND RECIPE (12 SLICES)

ingredients:
2 tsp. yeast
1 tsp. salt
2 tbsp. sugar
2 tbsp. nonfat dry milk powder
3 tbsp. wheat germ
1 cup whole wheat flour
2 cups bread flour
2 tbsp. apple butter
1 1/4 cups water
2 tbsp. orange marmalade

directions:
Add ingredients in the order suggested by the bread machine manufacturer and follow baking instructions provided in the manual.

Nutrition per Serving	1-Pound	1 1/2-Pound
Calories	129	129
Carbohydrate	27 grams	28 grams
Cholesterol	<1 milligram	<1 milligram
Dietary Fiber	3 grams	3 grams
Protein	5 grams	5 grams
Sodium	205 milligrams	184 milligrams

Exchanges

	1 2/3 starch	1 2/3 starch

ORANGE WHOLE WHEAT BREAD

1-POUND RECIPE (8 SLICES)

ingredients:
1 1/4 tsp. yeast
3/4 tsp. salt
1 tbsp. sugar
1 tbsp. nonfat dry milk powder
2 tbsp. wheat germ
3/4 cup whole wheat flour
1 1/4 cups bread flour
1 tsp. grated orange peel
2 tbsp. frozen orange juice concentrate, thawed
3/4 cup water

1 1/2-POUND RECIPE (12 SLICES)

ingredients:
2 tsp. yeast
1 1/4 tsp. salt
2 tbsp. sugar
2 tbsp. nonfat dry milk powder
3 tbsp. wheat germ
1 1/4 cups whole wheat flour
1 3/4 cups bread flour
1 1/2 tsp. grated orange peel
3 tbsp. frozen orange juice concentrate, thawed
1 cup + 3 tbsp. water

directions: Add ingredients in the order suggested by the bread machine manufacturer and follow baking instructions provided in the manual.

Nutrition per Serving	1-Pound	1 1/2-Pound
Calories	125	126
Carbohydrate	26 grams	26 grams
Cholesterol	<1 milligram	<1 milligram
Dietary Fiber	3 grams	3 grams
Protein	5 grams	5 grams
Sodium	206 milligrams	229 milligrams

Exchanges

	1-Pound	1 1/2-Pound
	1 2/3 starch	1 2/3 starch

PEACH BREAD

1-POUND RECIPE (8 SLICES)

ingredients:
1 1/2 tsp. yeast
1/4 tsp. salt
2 cups bread flour
2 tsp. cinnamon
1/4 cup sugar
1 1/2 tbsp. peach butter
1/4 cup egg substitute
3/4 cup skim milk

Filling:
1/2 cup peaches, diced
3 tbsp. brown sugar
1/2 tsp. almond extract
1/4 cup nonfat date and almond granola
(Health Valley)

1 1/2-POUND RECIPE (12 SLICES)

ingredients:
2 1/2 tsp. yeast
1/2 tsp. salt
3 cups bread flour
1 tbsp. cinnamon
1/3 cup sugar
2 tbsp. peach butter
1 egg white
1/4 cup egg substitute
1 cup skim milk

Continued on following page.

Continued from preceding page.

Filling:
2/3 cup peaches, diced
1/4 cup brown sugar
3/4 tsp. almond extract
1/3 cup nonfat date and almond granola
(Health Valley)

directions: Combine filling ingredients in small bowl; set aside. Add ingredients in the order suggested by the bread machine manufacturer and follow baking instructions provided in the manual.

Ten to 15 minutes before the rising period is over, stick fingers into dough to make in indentation for filling. Spoon the filling into the hole. Resume rising and baking process.

Nutrition per Serving	1-Pound	1 1/2-Pound
Calories	179	176
Carbohydrate	38 grams	36 grams
Cholesterol	<1 milligram	<1 milligram
Dietary Fiber	2 grams	2 grams
Protein	6 grams	6 grams
Sodium	93 milligrams	115 milligrams

Exchanges

	2 starch	2 starch
	1/2 fruit	1/2 fruit

PEACH-APRICOT BREAD

1-POUND RECIPE (8 SLICES)

ingredients:
1 tsp. yeast
1/2 tsp. salt
2 1/4 cups bread flour
1 tbsp. nonfat dry milk powder
1/2 tsp. sugar
1 cup water
1/4 cup dried peaches, chopped
1/4 cup apricots, chopped
1/2 tsp. cinnamon
3 tbsp. applesauce

1 1/2-POUND RECIPE (12 SLICES)

ingredients:
2 tsp. yeast
1 tsp. salt
3 1/4 cups bread flour
1 tbsp. nonfat dry milk powder
1 tsp. sugar
1 1/2 cups water
1/2 cup dried peaches, chopped
1/2 cup dried apricots, chopped
3/4 tsp. cinnamon
4 tbsp. applesauce

directions: Add ingredients in the order suggested by the bread manufacturer and follow baking instructions provided in the manual.

Nutrition per Serving	1-Pound	1 1/2-Pound
Calories	143	147
Carbohydrate	30 grams	31 grams
Cholesterol	<1 milligram	<1 milligram
Dietary Fiber	2 grams	3 grams
Protein	5 grams	5 grams
Sodium	140 milligrams	185 milligrams

Exchanges

	1 2/3 starch	1 2/3 starch
	1/3 fruit	1/3 fruit

PINEAPPLE BREAD

1-POUND RECIPE (8 SLICES)

ingredients:
1 1/4 tsp. yeast
1/2 tsp. salt
2 tbsp. nonfat dry milk powder
2 cups bread flour
2 tbsp. wheat bran
1 1/2 tsp. cinnamon
1 tbsp. frozen pineapple juice concentrate, thawed
1/2 cup pineapple chunks in juice, drained
1/3 cup water

1 1/2-POUND RECIPE (12 SLICES)

ingredients:
2 tsp. yeast
3/4 tsp. salt
3 tbsp. nonfat dry milk powder
3 cups bread flour
3 tbsp. wheat bran
2 tsp. cinnamon
1 1/2 tbsp. frozen pineapple juice concentrate, thawed
3/4 cup pineapple chunks in juice, drained
1/2 cup water

directions:
Add ingredients in the order suggested by the bread machine manufacturer and follow baking instructions provided in the manual.

Nutrition per Serving	1-Pound	1 1/2-Pound
Calories	119	119
Carbohydrate	24 grams	24 grams
Cholesterol	<1 milligram	<1 milligram
Dietary Fiber	2 grams	2 grams
Protein	4 grams	4 grams
Sodium	142 milligrams	142 milligrams

Exchanges

	1 1/3 starch	1 1/3 starch
	1/3 fruit	1/3 fruit

PINEAPPLE-SWEET POTATO BREAD

ingredients:
1-POUND RECIPE (8 SLICES)
1 1/2 tsp. yeast
1 tsp. salt
1/4 cup brown sugar
1 tsp. cinnamon
2 tbsp. wheat germ
2 cups bread flour
1/2 cup canned sweet potatoes, mashed
1/4 cup egg substitute
1/4 cup sugar-sweetened dry pineapple, chopped fine
1/3 cup water

ingredients:
1 1/2-POUND RECIPE (12 SLICES)
2 tsp. yeast
1 1/2 tsp. salt
1/3 cup brown sugar
2 tsp. cinnamon
3 tbsp. wheat germ
3 cups bread flour
3/4 cup canned sweet potatoes, mashed
1/4 cup egg substitute
1 egg white
1/3 cup sugar-sweetened dry pineapple, chopped fine
1/2 cup water

directions: Add ingredients in the order suggested by the bread machine manufacturer and follow baking instructions provided in the manual.

Nutrition per Serving	1-Pound	1 1/2-Pound
Calories	174	170
Carbohydrate	36 grams	35 grams
Cholesterol	0 milligrams	0 milligrams
Dietary Fiber	3 grams	2 grams
Protein	5 grams	5 grams
Sodium	284 milligrams	285 milligrams
Exchanges	1 2/3 starch	1 2/3 starch
	2/3 fruit	2/3 fruit

Kathleen Potrier, New Hampshire

84

PITA BREAD

8 PITA POCKETS

ingredients:
2 tsp. yeast
1/2 tsp. salt
2 tsp. dried basil
2 tsp. dried oregano
3/4 tsp. onion powder
1/4 tsp. garlic powder
1 1/2 cups bread flour
3/4 cup whole wheat flour
1 cup water

directions:
Add ingredients in the order suggested by the bread machine manufacturer and process on the dough cycle. Preheat oven to 500 degrees. Lightly spray baking sheets with nonfat cooking spray.
At the end of the dough cycle divide dough into 8 pieces.
On a surface sprinkled with flour, roll each piece until flattened into a thin circle. Place on prepared baking sheets and bake immediately, 15 minutes, or until pita is puffy and browned.

Nutrition per Serving	8 Pita Pockets
Calories	122
Carbohydrate	24 grams
Cholesterol	0 milligrams
Dietary Fiber	3 grams
Protein	5 grams
Sodium	136 milligrams

Exchanges

1 2/3 starch

PIZZA CRUST

SERVES 8

ingredients:
1 1/2 tsp. yeast
1 tsp. salt
1 1/4 cups + 1 1/2 tbsp. water
3 1/4 cups bread flour

directions:
Add ingredients in the order suggested by the bread machine manufacturer and process on the dough cycle.

When cycle is complete, remove dough from machine and divide into 6 equal portions. Roll each piece into a ball and place on a lightly-floured surface. Cover dough with plastic wrap or towel and let rest 20 minutes. Roll each ball on lightly-floured surface to form a flat circle.

Preheat oven to 500 degrees. Lightly spray baking sheet with nonfat cooking spray. Place flat circles onto prepared baking sheet and prick several times with a fork.

Add pizza sauce, cheese, and desired toppings. Bake in preheated oven 12 to 15 minutes, until cheese is melted and crust is golden brown.

*For thick crust pizza, use above recipe. Make 2 pizzas with above recipe for thin crust pizza.

Nutrition per Serving (crust only)	Serves 8
Calories	167
Carbohydrate	33 grams
Cholesterol	0 milligrams
Dietary Fiber	2 grams
Protein	6 grams
Sodium	270 milligrams

Exchanges

2 starch

POTATO BREAD

ingredients:

1-POUND RECIPE (8 SLICES)
1 1/2 tsp. yeast
3/4 tsp. salt
1 1/4 tbsp. sugar
3 tbsp. instant potato flakes
2 cups bread flour
1 1/2 tbsp. lite applesauce
3/4 cup skim milk
1 1/2 tbsp. water

ingredients:

1 1/2-POUND RECIPE (12 SLICES)
2 1/2 tsp. yeast
1 tsp. salt
1 3/4 tbsp. sugar
1/4 cup instant potato flakes
3 cups bread flour
1 tbsp. lite applesauce
1 cup skim milk
2 1/2 tbsp. water

directions: Add ingredients in the order suggested by the bread machine manufacturer and follow baking instructions provided in the manual.

Nutrition per Serving	1-Pound	1 1/2-Pound
Calories	125	125
Carbohydrate	25 grams	25 grams
Cholesterol	<1 milligram	<1 milligram
Dietary Fiber	2 grams	2 grams
Protein	5 grams	5 grams
Sodium	214 milligrams	191 milligrams

Exchanges

	1 2/3 starch	1 2/3 starch

PRUNE BREAD

1-POUND RECIPE (8 SLICES)

ingredients: 1 1/2 tsp. yeast
3/4 tsp. salt
1/2 tsp. cinnamon
1/4 cup nonfat dry milk powder
1/2 cup bran
1/2 cup whole wheat flour
1 1/2 cups bread flour
2 tbsp. molasses
2 tbsp. Lighter Bake
1 cup prune juice
1/2 cup chopped prunes

1 1/2-POUND RECIPE (12 SLICES)

ingredients: 2 1/2 tsp. yeast
1 tsp. salt
3/4 tsp. cinnamon
1/3 cup nonfat dry milk powder
2/3 cup bran
2/3 cup whole wheat flour
2 cups bread flour
3 tbsp. molasses
3 tbsp. Lighter Bake
1 1/3 cups prune juice
3/4 cup chopped prunes

directions: Add ingredients in the order suggested by the bread machine manufacturer and follow baking instructions provided in the manual.
Add chopped prunes during the raisin-bread cycle or 5 minutes before kneading is finished.

Nutrition per Serving	1-Pound	1 1/2-Pound
Calories	187	172
Carbohydrate	41 grams	38 grams
Cholesterol	<1 milligram	<1 milligram
Dietary Fiber	4 grams	3 grams
Protein	6 grams	5 grams
Sodium	221 milligrams	197 milligrams
Exchanges	2 starch	1 2/3 starch
	2/3 fruit	2/3 fruit

PUMPERNICKEL BREAD

ingredients: **1-POUND RECIPE (8 SLICES)**
1 tsp. yeast
3/4 tsp. salt
1 tbsp. nonfat dry milk powder
2 tbsp. unsweetened cocoa powder
2 cups bread flour
1/4 cup rye flour
1/4 cup + 3 tbsp. whole wheat flour
1 tbsp. apple butter
2 tbsp. molasses
1 cup water

ingredients: **1 1/2-POUND RECIPE (12 SLICES)**
1 1/2 tsp. yeast
1 1/2 tsp. salt
2 tbsp. nonfat dry milk powder
3 tbsp. unsweetened cocoa powder
3 1/4 cups bread flour
1/2 cup rye flour
1/3 cup whole wheat flour
2 tbsp. apple butter
3 tbsp. molasses
1 1/2 cups + 1 tbsp. water

directions: Add ingredients in the order suggested by the bread machine manufactuer and follow baking instructions provided in the manual.

Nutrition per Serving	1-Pound	1 1/2-Pound
Calories	158	162
Carbohydrate	32 grams	36 grams
Cholesterol	<1 milligram	<1 milligram
Dietary Fiber	2 grams	2 grams
Protein	5 grams	5 grams
Sodium	232 milligrams	276 milligrams

Exchanges

	2 starch	2 starch

PUMPKIN-RAISIN BREAD

ingredients: **1-POUND RECIPE (8 SLICES)**
1 tsp. yeast
3/4 tsp. salt
1 tbsp. sugar
3/4 tsp. pumpkin pie spice
1 tbsp. nonfat dry milk powder
2 3/4 cups bread flour
1/4 cup Lighter Bake
1/4 cup pumpkin purée
3/4 cup water
1/4 cup raisins

ingredients: **1 1/2-POUND RECIPE (12 SLICES)**
1 1/2 tsp. yeast
1 tsp. salt
2 tbsp. sugar
1 tsp. pumpkin pie spice
2 tbsp. nonfat dry milk powder
3 1/4 cups bread flour
1/4 cup + 2 tbsp. Lighter Bake
1/3 cup pumpkin purée
1 cup water
1/3 cup raisins

directions: Add ingredients in the order suggested by the bread machine manufacturer and follow baking instructions provided in the manual.

Nutrition per Serving	1-Pound	1 1/2-Pound
Calories	182	154
Carbohydrate	38 grams	33 grams
Cholesterol	0 milligrams	>1 milligram
Dietary Fiber	2 grams	2 grams
Protein	5 grams	4 grams
Sodium	210 milligrams	188 milligrams

Exchanges

	1-Pound	1 1/2-Pound
	1 2/3 starch	1 1/3 starch
	1 fruit	1 fruit

RAISIN BRAN MUFFIN BREAD

1-POUND RECIPE (8 SLICES)

ingredients:
1 tsp. yeast
1/4 tsp. salt
1/2 cup wheat bran
1/2 cup whole wheat flour
1 1/2 cups bread flour
1 1/2 tbsp. Lighter Bake
2 tbsp. egg substitute
2/3 cup water
1/2 cup raisins

1 1/2 POUND RECIPE (12 SLICES)

ingredients:
1 1/2 tsp. yeast
1/2 tsp. salt
3/4 cup wheat bran
1 cup whole wheat flour
2 cups bread flour
2 tbsp. Lighter Bake
1/4 cup egg substitute
1 cup water
3/4 cup raisins

directions: Add ingredients in the order suggested by the bread machine manufacturer and follow baking instructions provided in the manual.

Nutrition per Serving	1-Pound	1 1/2-Pound
Calories	145	146
Carbohydrate	32 grams	32 grams
Cholesterol	0 milligrams	0 milligrams
Dietary Fiber	3 grams	3 grams
Protein	5 grams	5 grams
Sodium	72 milligrams	100 milligrams

Exchanges

	1 2/3 starch	1 2/3 starch

RAISIN-CINNAMON CRANBERRY-BANANA BREAD

ingredients:
1-POUND RECIPE (8 SLICES)
1 tsp. yeast
1/2 tsp. salt
3/4 tsp. cinnamon
2 1/4 cups bread flour
1 tbsp. nonfat dry milk powder
1/2 tsp. sugar
2 tbsp. lite applesauce
1/2 cup mashed bananas
1 cup water
1/4 cup cranberries
1/4 cup raisins

ingredients:
1 1/2-POUND RECIPE (12 SLICES)
2 tsp. yeast
1 tsp. salt
1 tsp. cinnamon
3 1/4 cups bread flour
2 tbsp. nonfat dry milk powder
1 tsp. sugar
1/4 cup lite applesauce
3/4 cup mashed bananas
1 1/2 cups water
1/3 cup cranberries
1/3 cup raisins

directions: Add ingredients in the order suggested by the bread machine manufacturer and follow baking instructions provided in the manual.

Nutrition per Serving	1-Pound	1 1/2-Pound
Calories	142	139
Carbohydrate	30 grams	29 grams
Cholesterol	<1 milligram	<1 milligram
Dietary Fiber	2 grams	2 grams
Protein	5 grams	5 grams
Sodium	140 milligrams	185 milligrams
Exchanges	1 2/3 starch	1 2/3 starch
	1/3 fruit	1/3 fruit

RAISIN OATMEAL BREAD

1-POUND RECIPE (8 SLICES)

ingredients:
1 tsp. yeast
1/4 tsp. salt
3/4 tsp. cinnamon
1/4 cup multi-grain oatmeal
2 cups bread flour
2 tbsp. apple butter
3/4 cup water
2 tbsp. lite applesauce
1/4 cup raisins

1 1/2-POUND RECIPE (12 SLICES)

ingredients:
1 1/2 tsp. yeast
1/2 tsp. salt
1 tsp. cinnamon
1/3 cup multi-grain oatmeal
3 cups bread flour
3 tbsp. apple butter
1 cup water
1/3 cup lite applesauce
1/3 cup raisins

directions: Add ingredients in the order suggested by the bread machine manufacturer and follow baking instructions provided in the manual.

Nutrition per Serving	1-Pound	1 1/2-Pound
Calories:	136	135
Carbohydrate	29 grams	28 grams
Cholesterol	0 milligrams	0 milligrams
Dietary Fiber	2 grams	2 grams
Protein	4 grams	4 grams
Sodium	70 milligrams	92 milligrams

Exchanges

	1 1/3 starch	1 1/3 starch
	1/2 fruit	1/2 fruit

RAISIN RYE BREAD

1-POUND RECIPE (8 SLICES)

ingredients: 1 1/2 tsp. yeast
1/2 tsp. salt
1 1/2 tbsp. brown sugar
1 1/4 cups bread flour
1/2 cup whole wheat flour
1/2 cup rye flour
1 tbsp. honey
1 1/2 tbsp. Lighter Bake
3/8 cup skim milk
3/8 cup water
1 1/2 tbsp. raisins

1 1/2-POUND RECIPE (12 SLICES)

ingredients: 2 tsp. yeast
3/4 tsp. salt
2 tbsp. brown sugar
1 3/4 cups bread flour
1 cup whole wheat flour
3/4 cup rye flour
1 1/2 tbsp. honey
2 tbsp. Lighter Bake
5/8 cup skim milk
5/8 cup water
2 tbsp. raisins

directions: Place milk, water, Lighter Bake, honey, raisins and brown sugar in food processor or blender and process until blended and smooth.
Add dry ingredients and blended mixture in the order suggested by the bread machine manufacturer and follow baking instructions provided in the manual.

Nutrition per Serving	1-Pound	1 1/2-Pound
Calories	151	153
Carbohydrate	32 grams	33 grams
Cholesterol	<1 milligram	<1 milligram
Dietary Fiber	2 grams	3 grams
Protein	5 grams	5 grams
Sodium	43 milligrams	144 milligrams

Exchanges

	1 2/3 starch	1 2/3 starch
	1/2 fruit	1/2 fruit

RASPBERRY BREAD

1-POUND RECIPE (8 SLICES)

ingredients:
1 tsp. yeast
1/2 tsp. salt
1/2 tsp. sugar
1 tbsp. nonfat dry milk powder
2 1/4 cups bread flour
1/2 cup multi-grain oatmeal
2 tbsp. lite applesauce
1/4 cup raspberries, mashed
3/4 cup water

1 1/2-POUND RECIPE (12 SLICES)

ingredients:
1/2 tsp. yeast
3/4 tsp. salt
1 tsp. sugar
2 tbsp. nonfat dry milk powder
3 cups bread flour
1 cup multi-grain oatmeal
3 tbsp. lite applesauce
1/2 cup raspberries, mashed
1 cup water

directions: Add ingredients in the order suggested by the bread machine manufacturer and follow baking instructions provided in the manual.

Nutrition per Serving	1-Pound	1 1/2-Pound
Calories	138	132
Carbohydrate	28 grams	27 grams
Cholesterol	<1 milligram	<1 milligram
Dietary Fiber	2 grams	2 grams
Protein	5 grams	5 grams
Sodium	140 milligrams	141 milligrams

Exchanges

	1 2/3 starch	1 2/3 starch

RASPBERRY CHEESE BREAD

1-POUND RECIPE (8 SLICES)

ingredients:
1 3/4 tsp. yeast
1 cup bread flour
1/2 cup multi-grain oatmeal
2 tbsp. honey
1 tbsp. lite applesauce
1/4 cup nonfat cream cheese
1/4 cup raspberries, mashed
1/4 cup skim milk

1 1/2-POUND RECIPE (12 SLICES)

ingredients:
2 1/2 tsp. yeast
2 cups bread flour
1 cup multi-grain oatmeal
3 tbsp. honey
2 tbsp. lite applesauce
1/2 cup nonfat cream cheese
1/2 cup raspberries, mashed
1/2 cup skim milk

directions: Add ingredients in the order suggested by the bread machine manufacturer and follow baking instructions provided in the manual.

Nutrition per Serving	1-Pound	1 1/2-Pound
Calories	169	168
Carbohydrate	34 grams	33 grams
Cholesterol	<1 milligram	<1 milligram
Dietary Fiber	3 grams	3 grams
Protein	7 grams	7 grams
Sodium	70 milligrams	86 milligrams

Exchanges

	2 1/3 starch	2 1/2 starch

RICH WHITE BREAD

1-POUND RECIPE (8 SLICES)

ingredients:
1 1/2 tsp. yeast
2 cups bread flour
3 tbsp. sugar
1 tbsp. low-fat margarine
1 tbsp. fat-free margarine
1/4 cup egg substitute
3/4 cup skim milk

1 1/2-POUND RECIPE (12 SLICES)

ingredients:
2 1/2 tsp. yeast
3 cups bread flour
1/4 cup sugar
1 1/2 tbsp. low-fat margarine
1 tbsp. fat-free margarine
1 egg white
1/4 cup egg substitute
1 cup skim milk

directions: Add ingredients in the order suggested by the bread machine manufacturer and follow baking instructions provided in the manual.

Nutrition per Serving	1-Pound	1 1/2-Pound
Calories	136	134
Carbohydrate	26 grams	26 grams
Cholesterol	<1 gram	<1 gram
Dietary Fiber	2 grams	2 grams
Protein	5 grams	5 grams
Sodium	49 milligrams	45 milligrams

Exchanges

	1-Pound	1 1/2-Pound
	1 2/3 starch	1 2/3 starch

ROASTED GARLIC BREAD

1-POUND RECIPE (8 SLICES)

ingredients:
1 1/4 tsp. yeast
1/2 tsp. salt
1 tbsp. sugar
2 cups bread flour
1/4 cup Fat-free Roasted Garlic Dressing
2/3 cup water

1 1/2-POUND RECIPE (12 SLICES)

ingredients:
1 3/4 tsp. yeast
3/4 tsp. salt
2 tbsp. sugar
3 cups bread flour
1/3 cup Fat-free Roasted Garlic Dressing
1 cup water

directions: Add ingredients in the order suggested by the bread machine manufacturer and follow baking instructions provided in the manual.

Nutrition per Serving	1-Pound	1 1/2-Pound
Calories	114	116
Carbohydrate	23 grams	23 grams
Cholesterol	0 milligrams	0 milligrams
Dietary Fiber	1 gram	1 gram
Protein	4 grams	4 grams
Sodium	166 milligrams	164 milligrams

Exchanges

	1 1/3 starch	1 1/3 starch

RYE BREAD

1-POUND RECIPE (8 SLICES)

ingredients: 1 1/2 tsp. yeast
1/4 tsp. salt
2 tbsp. nonfat dry milk powder
1 1/2 cups bread flour
3/4 cup rye flour
1/4 cup apple butter
2/3 cup water

1 1/2-POUND RECIPE (12 SLICES)

ingredients: 2 1/4 tsp. yeast
1/2 tsp. salt
3 tbsp. nonfat dry milk powder
2 cups bread flour
1 1/4 cups rye flour
1/3 cup apple butter
1 cup water

directions: Add ingredients in the order suggested by the bread machine manufacturer and follow baking instructions provided in the manual.

Nutrition per Serving	1-Pound	1 1/2-Pound
Calories	140	134
Carbohydrate	29 grams	28 grams
Cholesterol	<1 milligram	<1 milligram
Dietary Fiber	2 grams	2 grams
Protein	5 grams	5 grams
Sodium	74 milligrams	96 milligrams

Exchanges

	1-Pound	1 1/2-Pound
	1 2/3 starch	1 2/3 starch
	1/3 fruit	1/3 fruit

SEEDED RYE BREAD

1-POUND RECIPE (8 SLICES)

ingredients:
1 1/4 tsp. yeast
3/4 tsp. salt
1/4 tsp. caraway seeds
1 tbsp. sugar
1 tbsp. nonfat dry milk powder
1/2 cup rye flour
1 1/2 cups bread flour
2 tsp. Lighter Bake
3/4 cup water

1 1/2-POUND RECIPE (12 SLICES)

ingredients:
2 1/4 tsp. yeast
1 tsp. salt
3/4 tsp. caraway seeds
2 tbsp. sugar
2 tbsp. nonfat dry milk powder
3/4 cup rye flour
2 1/2 cups bread flour
1 tbsp. Lighter Bake
1 cup + 3 tbsp. water

directions: Add ingredients in the order suggested by the bread machine manufacturer and follow baking instructions provided in the manual.

Nutrition per Serving	1-Pound	1 1/2-Pound
Calories	115	128
Carbohydrate	23 grams	26 grams
Cholesterol	<1 milligram	<1 milligram
Dietary Fiber	1 gram	2 grams
Protein	4 grams	5 grams
Sodium	205 milligrams	186 milligrams

Exchanges

	1 1/3 starch	1 2/3 starch

SEEDY ONION BREAD

ingredients:

1-POUND RECIPE (8 SLICES)

1 1/2 tsp. yeast
1 tsp. salt
3/4 tsp. onion powder
3/4 tsp. minced onion flakes
1 tsp. poppy seeds
1 tsp. sesame seeds
1 tbsp. sugar
2 cups bread flour
3/4 tbsp. low-fat margarine
1/4 tbsp. fat-free margarine
1 cup water

ingredients:

1 1/2-POUND RECIPE (12 SLICES)

2 1/2 tsp. yeast
1 1/2 tsp. salt
1 tsp. onion powder
1 tsp. minced onion flakes
1 1/2 tsp. poppy seeds
1 1/2 tsp. sesame seeds
1 1/2 tbsp. sugar
3 cups bread flour
1 tbsp. low-fat margarine
1/2 tbsp. fat-free margarine
1 1/2 cups water

directions: Add ingredients in the order suggested by the bread machine manufacturer and follow baking instructions provided in the manual.

Nutrition per Serving	1-Pound	1 1/2-Pound
Calories	117	117
Carbohydrate	22 grams	22 grams
Cholesterol	0 milligrams	0 milligrams
Dietary Fiber	2 grams	2 grams
Protein	4 grams	4 grams
Sodium	282 milligrams	282 milligrams

Exchanges

	1 1/3 starch	1 1/3 starch

SIMPLE MIX BREAD

1-POUND RECIPE (8 SLICES)

ingredients: 1 1/2 tsp. yeast
2 1/4 cups Bread Mix*
1 tbsp. lite applesauce
3/4 cup warm water

1 1/2-POUND RECIPE (12 SLICES)

ingredients: 2 tsp. yeast
3 1/3 cups Bread Mix*
1 1/2 tbsp. lite applesauce
1 1/4 cups warm water

directions: Add ingredients in the order suggested by the bread machine manufacturer and follow baking instructions provided in the manual.
*Use Bread Mix provided.

Nutrition per Serving	1-Pound	1 1/2-Pound
Calories	119	117
Carbohydrate	24 grams	23 grams
Cholesterol	<1 milligram	<1 milligram
Dietary Fiber	2 grams	2 grams
Protein	4 grams	4 grams
Sodium	263 milligrams	260 milligrams

Exchanges

	1-Pound	1 1/2-Pound
	1 1/3 starch	1 1/3 starch
	1/3 fruit	1/3 fruit

Susan Melton, South Carolina

SIMPLE WHITE BREAD

1-POUND RECIPE (8 SLICES)

ingredients: 1 1/2 tsp. yeast
1 tsp. salt
2 cups bread flour
1 1/2 tbsp. sugar
1 cup water

1 1/2-POUND RECIPE (12 SLICES)

ingredients: 2 1/2 tsp. yeast
1 1/2 tsp. salt
3 cups bread flour
2 tbsp. sugar
1 1/2 cups water

directions: Add ingredients in the order suggested by the bread machine manufacturer and follow baking instructions provided in the manual.

Nutrition per Serving	1-Pound	1 1/2-Pound
Calories	112	112
Carbohydrate	23 grams	23 grams
Cholesterol	0 milligrams	0 milligrams
Dietary Fiber	2 grams	2 grams
Protein	4 grams	4 grams
Sodium	269 milligrams	269 milligrams

Exchanges

	1 1/3 starch	1 1/3 starch

SIMPLY WHITE BREAD

1-POUND RECIPE (8 SLICES)

ingredients: 1 tsp. yeast
1/2 tsp. salt
2 cups bread flour
1 tbsp. nonfat dry milk powder
2 tbsp. sugar
1/2 tbsp. low-fat margarine
1/2 tbsp. fat-free margarine
3/4 cup water

1 1/2-POUND RECIPE (12 SLICES)

ingredients: 1 1/2 tsp. yeast
3/4 tsp. salt
3 cups bread flour
1 1/2 tbsp. nonfat dry milk powder
3 tbsp. sugar
1 tbsp. low-fat margarine
1/2 tbsp. fat-free margarine
1 1/4 cups water

directions: Add ingredients in the order suggested by the bread machine manufacturer and follow baking instructions provided in the manual.

Nutrition per Serving	1-Pound	1 1/2-Pound
Calories	118	118
Carbohydrate	24 grams	24 grams
Cholesterol	<1 milligram	<1 milligram
Dietary Fiber	1 gram	1 gram
Protein	4 grams	4 grams
Sodium	151 milligrams	151 milligrams

Exchanges

	1 1/3 starch	1 1/3 starch
	1/3 fruit	1/3 fruit

SOURDOUGH STARTER

ingredients: 2 cups bread flour
1 cup skin milk, warmed
1 cup water, warmed
2 tsp. yeast
1 tsp. sugar

directions: Combine all ingredients in a medium bowl and
beat with electric mixer until smooth. Cover the
bowl with a towel and leave in a warm place for 5
to 7 days, stirring mixture once a day. The starter
is ready when it becomes frothy and has a sour
smell. (Throw away any mixture that becomes
pinkish in color or has an overly sour smell.) Store
leftover starter in a tightly-sealed jar in the refrigerator. This starter can be renewed by adding 1/2
cup water, 1/2 cup skim milk, and 1 cup flour after
each use. The starter must be used after 7 to 14 days
or can be well-kept by removing 1 cupful every 7
to 10 days and replenishing the mixture with the
water, milk and flour (as described above).

<u>**Nutrition per Serving (24)**</u>
Calories	46
Carbohydrate	9 grams
Cholesterol	0 milligrams
Dietary Fiber	<1 gram
Protein	2 grams
Sodium	35 milligrams

SOUTHWEST ZUCCHINI BREAD

1-POUND RECIPE (8 SLICES)

ingredients: 1 1/4 tsp. yeast
1/4 tsp. salt
1 tsp. ground cumin
1/8 tsp. cayenne pepper
1/4 cup cornmeal
2 cups bread flour
1/2 cup grated zucchini
1/2 cup lite applesauce
1/4 cup water
1/2 cup chopped dates

1 1/2-POUND RECIPE (12 SLICES)

ingredients: 2 tsp. yeast
1/2 tsp. salt
1 1/2 tsp. ground cumin
1/3 tsp. cayenne pepper
1/3 cup cornmeal
3 cups bread flour
3/4 cup grated zucchini
1/2 cup lite applesauce
1/2 cup water
3/4 cup chopped dates

directions: Add ingredients in the order suggested by the bread machine manufacturer and follow baking instructions provided in the manual.

Nutrition per Serving	1-Pound	1 1/2-Pound
Calories	159	155
Carbohydrate	34 grams	33 grams
Cholesterol	0 milligrams	0 milligrams
Dietary Fiber	3 grams	3 grams
Protein	5 grams	5 grams
Sodium	70 milligrams	93 milligrams
Exchanges	1 starch	1 starch
	1 vegetable	1 vegetable
	1 fruit	1 fruit

SPICE-CARROT BREAD

1-POUND RECIPE (8 SLICES)

ingredients: 1 tsp. yeast
2 3/4 cups bread flour
1 tbsp. nonfat dry milk powder
1 tbsp. apple butter
2 tbsp. grated carrots
3/4 tbsp. allspice
1 tbsp. honey
3/4 cup water

1 1/2-POUND RECIPE (12 SLICES)

ingredients: 1 1/2 tsp. yeast
3 1/4 cups bread flour
2 tbsp. nonfat dry milk powder
2 tbsp. apple butter
1/4 cups grated carrots
1 tbsp. allspice
2 tbsp. honey
1 cup water

directions: Add ingredients in the order suggested by the bread machine manufacturer and follow baking instructions provided in the manual.

Nutrition per Serving	1-Pound	1 1/2-Pound
Calories	157	133
Carbohydrate	32 grams	27 grams
Cholesterol	<1 milligram	<1 milligram
Dietary fiber	2 grams	2 grams
Protein	5 grams	4 grams
Sodium	7 milligrams	8 milligrams

Exchanges

	1 2/3 starch	1 1/3 starch
	1/2 fruit	1/2 fruit

SPICED HONEY BREAD

ingredients:

1-POUND RECIPE (8 SLICES)
1 1/2 tsp. yeast
1/2 tsp. salt
1/2 tsp. cinnamon
1/2 tsp. ginger
2 1/4 cups bread flour
1 1/2 tbsp. apple butter
1 1/2 tbsp. lite applesauce
3 tbsp. honey
2 tbsp. skim milk
3/4 cup water

ingredients:

1 1/2-POUND RECIPE (12 SLICES)
2 1/2 tsp. yeast
3/4 tsp. salt
1 tsp. cinnamon
1 tsp. ginger
3 cups bread flour
2 tbsp. apple butter
2 tbsp. lite applesauce
1/4 cup honey
3 tbsp. skim milk
1 cup water

directions: Add ingredients in the order suggested by the bread machine manufacturer and follow baking instructions provided in the manual.

Nutrition per Serving	1-Pound	1 1/2-Pound
Calories	151	136
Carbohydrate	32 grams	28 grams
Cholesterol	<1 milligram	<1 milligram
Dietary Fiber	2 grams	2 grams
Protein	5 grams	4 grams
Sodium	138 milligrams	138 milligrams

Exchanges

	1-Pound	1 1/2-Pound
	1 2/3 starch	1 1/3 starch
	1/2 fruit	1/2 fruit

SPICY CAJUN-SEASONED BREAD

1-POUND RECIPE (8 SLICES)

ingredients:
1 tsp. yeast
1 tbsp. nonfat dry milk powder
1/2 tsp. salt
1 tsp. Spicy Cajun seasoning
1 tbsp. sugar
2 cups bread flour
1/2 tsp. garlic powder
1 tbsp. onion powder
2 tsp. lite applesauce
3/4 cup water

1 1/2-POUND RECIPE (12 SLICES)

ingredients:
1 3/4 tsp. yeast
2 tbsp. nonfat dry milk powder
3/4 tsp. salt
2 tsp. Spicy Cajun seasoning
2 tbsp. sugar
3 cups bread flour
1 tsp. garlic powder
1 1/2 tbsp. onion powder
1 tbsp. lite applesauce
1 cup water

directions: Add ingredients in the order suggested by the bread machine manufacturer and follow baking instructions provided in the manual.

Nutrition per Serving	1-Pound	1 1/2-Pound
Calories	112	115
Carbohydrate	23 grams	23 grams
Cholesterol	0 milligrams	0 milligrams
Dietary Fiber	1 gram	1 gram
Protein	4 grams	4 grams
Sodium	136 milligrams	136 milligrams

Exchanges

	1 1/3 starch	1 1/3 starch

STRAWBERRY BREAD

1-POUND RECIPE (8 SLICES)

ingredients:
1 1/2 tsp. yeast
3/4 tsp. salt
1/4 cup sugar
2 tbsp. nonfat dry milk powder
3/4 tsp. cinnamon
2 1/2 cups bread flour
1/4 cup egg substitute
1/3 cup water
2/3 cups strawberries, chopped

1 1/2-POUND RECIPE (12 SLICES)

ingredients:
2 tsp. yeast
1 tsp. salt
1/3 cup sugar
3 tbsp. nonfat dry milk powder
1 1/2 tsp. cinnamon
3 1/4 cups bread flour
1/2 cup egg substitute
1/2 cup water
1 cup strawberries, chopped

directions: Add ingredients in the order suggested by the bread machine manufacturer and follow baking instructions provided in the manual.

Nutrition per Serving	1-Pound	1 1/2-Pound
Calories	179	161
Carbohydrate	38 grams	34 grams
Cholesterol	<1 milligram	<1 milligram
Dietary Fiber	3 grams	3 grams
Protein	6 grams	5 grams
Sodium	219 milligrams	200 milligrams

Exchanges

	1-Pound	1 1/2-Pound
	2 starch	1 2/3 starch
	1/3 fruit	2/3 fruit

Kathleen Poirier, New Hampshire

SUB SANDWICH ROLLS

8 ROLLS

ingredients:
1 1/4 tsp. yeast
1/2 tsp. salt
2 tbsp. nonfat dry milk powder
1 1/2 cups bread flour
3/4 cup whole wheat flour
3/4 cup + 2 tbsp. water

directions:
Add ingredients in the order suggested by the bread machine manufacturer and process on the dough cycle.

At the end of the dough cycle, remove from the machine.

Cut dough into 8 equal pieces.

On a lightly-floured surface, roll each piece into about a 6-inch rope.

Lightly spray a nonstick baking sheet with nonfat cooking spray. Place rolls 2 to 3 inches apart on baking sheet, cover, and let rise until doubled in size, about 20 to 30 minutes.

Preheat oven to 350 degrees.

When rolls are finished rising, bake 20 to 25 minutes, until lightly browned.

Nutrition per Serving

Calories	121
Carbohydrate	24 grams
Cholesterol	<1 milligram
Dietary Fiber	3 grams
Protein	5 grams
Sodium	141 milligrams

Exchanges

1 2/3 starch

SWEET CORNBREAD

1-POUND RECIPE (8 SLICES)

ingredients:
1 tsp. yeast
1/2 tsp. salt
1 tbsp. nonfat dry milk powder
2 1/4 cups bread flour
1/4 cup cornmeal
2 tbsp. lite applesauce
1 tbsp. honey
3/4 cup water

1 1/2-POUND RECIPE (12 SLICES)

ingredients:
1 1/2 tsp. yeast
3/4 tsp. salt
1 1/2 tbsp. nonfat dry milk powder
3 1/3 cups bread flour
1/3 cup cornmeal
2 1/2 tbsp. lite applesauce
1 1/2 tbsp. honey
1 cup + 2 1/2 tbsp. water

directions:
Add ingredients in the order suggested by the bread machine manufacturer and follow baking instructions provided in the manual.

Nutrition per Serving	1-Pound	1 1/2-Pound
Calories	143	139
Carbohydrate	29 grams	28 grams
Cholesterol	<1 milligram	<1 milligram
Dietary Fiber	2 grams	2 grams
Protein	5 grams	5 grams
Sodium	139 milligrams	139 milligrams

Exchanges

	1 2/3 starch	1 2/3 starch
	1/3 fruit	1/3 fruit

SWEET DOUGH

1-POUND RECIPE (8 SLICES)

ingredients: 1 1/2 tsp. yeast
1/2 tsp. salt
1 tbsp. sugar
1 tbsp. nonfat dry milk powder
2 cups all-purpose flour
1/4 cup egg substitute
2 tbsp. lite applesauce
1/2 cup water

1 1/2-POUND RECIPE (12 SLICES)

ingredients: 1 1/2 tsp. yeast
3/4 tsp. salt
2 tbsp. sugar
2 tbsp. nonfat dry milk powder
3 cups all-purpose flour
1/4 cup egg substitute
3 tbsp. lite applesauce
3/4 cup water

directions: Add ingredients in the order suggested by the bread machine manufacturer and process on the dough cycle.
Remove dough from machine and use for recipes requiring Sweet Dough (Cinnamon Rolls, Sticky Buns, Cinnamon-Sugar Bubble Bread, Apple Strudel).

Nutrition per Serving	1-Pound	1 1/2-Pound
Calories	130	130
Carbohydrate	27 grams	27 grams
Cholesterol	<1 milligram	<1 milligram
Dietary Fiber	1 gram	1 gram
Protein	5 grams	4 grams
Sodium	147 milligrams	145 milligrams

Exchanges

	1 2/3 starch	1 2/3 starch

SWEET OATMEAL BREAD

1-POUND RECIPE (8 SLICES)

ingredients:
1 1/2 tsp. yeast
3/4 tsp. salt
1 cup multi-grain oatmeal
1 1/2 cups bread flour
1 tbsp. Lighter Bake
2 tbsp. honey
1/2 cup egg substitute
1 cup skim milk

1 1/2-POUND RECIPE (12 SLICES)

ingredients:
2 1/2 tsp. yeast
1 tsp. salt
1 1/2 cups multi-grain oatmeal
2 cups bread flour
2 tbsp. Lighter Bake
3 tbsp. honey
3/4 cup egg substitute
1 1/3 cups skim milk

directions:
Add ingredients in the order suggested by the bread machine manufacturer and follow baking instructions provided in the manual.

Nutrition per Serving	1-Pound	1 1/2-Pound
Calories	149	141
Carbohydrate	30 grams	28 grams
Cholesterol	<1 milligram	<1 milligram
Dietary Fiber	3 grams	2 grams
Protein	7 grams	6 grams
Sodium	241 milligrams	217 milligrams

Exchanges

	2 starch	2 starch

SWEET POTATO BREAD

1-POUND RECIPE (8 SLICES)

ingredients:
2 tsp. yeast
2 cups bread flour
2 tbsp. sugar
3/4 tsp. cinnamon
1/2 tsp. nutmeg
3 tbsp. molasses
1 tbsp. lite applesauce
1 tbsp. Lighter Bake
3/4 cup canned sweet potatoes,
drained and mashed
1/4 cup skim milk

1 1/2- POUND RECIPE (12 SLICES)

ingredients:
2 1/2 tsp. yeast
3 cups bread flour
3 tbsp. sugar
1 tsp. cinnamon
3/4 tsp. nutmeg
1/4 cup molasses
2 tbsp. lite applesauce
2 tbsp. Lighter Bake
1 cup canned sweet potatoes,
drained and mashed
1/2 cup skim milk

directions:
Add ingredients in the order suggested by the bread machine manufacturer and follow baking instructions provided in the manual.

Nutrition per Serving	1-Pound	1 1/2-Pound
Calories	167	164
Carbohydrate	35 grams	35 grams
Cholesterol	<1 milligram	<1 milligram
Dietary Fiber	2 grams	2 grams
Protein	5 grams	5 grams
Sodium	32 milligrams	31 milligrams

Exchanges

	1 2/3 starch	1 2/3 starch
	2/3 fruit	2/3 fruit

115

SWEET POTATO-RAISIN BREAD

1-POUND RECIPE (8 SLICES)

ingredients:
3/4 tsp. yeast
1/2 tsp. salt
3/4 tsp. cinnamon
1/2 tsp. nutmeg
2 tbsp. brown sugar
2 cups bread flour
1 tbsp. apple butter
1/3 cup + 2 tbsp. water
1/2 cup canned sweet potatoes,
drained and mashed
1/3 cup raisins

1 1/2-POUND RECIPE (12 SLICES)

ingredients:
1 tsp. yeast
1 tsp. salt
1 tsp. cinnamon
3/4 tsp. nutmeg
3 tbsp. brown sugar
3 cups bread flour
1 tbsp. apple butter
2/3 cup water
3/4 cup canned sweet potatoes, drained and
mashed
1/2 cup raisins

directions:
Add ingredients in the order suggested by the bread machine manufacturer and follow baking instructions provided in the manual.

Nutrition per Serving	1-Pound	1 1/2-Pound
Calories	155	153
Carbohydrate	33 grams	33 grams
Cholesterol	0 milligrams	0 milligrams
Dietary Fiber	2 grams	2 grams
Protein	4 grams	4 grams
Sodium	149 milligrams	149 milligrams
Exchanges	1 1/3 starch	1 1/3 starch
	1 fruit	1 fruit

116

WHEAT BRAN BREAD

1-POUND RECIPE (8 SLICES)

ingredients:
1 tsp. yeast
1 tsp. salt
1 tbsp. nonfat dry milk powder
1 3/4 cups whole wheat flour
3/4 cup bread flour
1 1/2 tbsp. brown sugar
2 tbsp. wheat bran
1 tbsp. apple butter
1 cup water

1 1/2-POUND RECIPE (12 SLICES)

ingredients:
1 1/2 tsp. yeast
1 1/2 tsp. salt
2 tbsp. nonfat dry milk powder
2 1/4 cups whole wheat flour
1 cup bread flour
2 1/2 tbsp. brown sugar
1/4 cup wheat bran
2 tbsp. apple butter
1 1/2 cups water

directions:
Add ingredients in the order suggested by the bread machine manufacturer and follow instructions provided in the manual.

Nutrition per Serving	1-Pound	1 1/2-Pound
Calories	147	139
Carbohydrate	31 grams	29 grams
Cholesterol	<1 milligram	<1 milligram
Dietary Fiber	4 grams	4 grams
Protein	6 grams	5 grams
Sodium	272 milligrams	273 milligrams

Exchanges

	2 starch	1 2/3 starch

117

WHITE BREAD

1-POUND RECIPE (8 SLICES)

ingredients:
1 1/2 tsp. yeast
3/4 tsp. salt
2 1/2 cups bread flour
2 tbsp. sugar
1/4 cup egg substitute
1 cup nonfat sour cream

1 1/2-POUND RECIPE (12 SLICES)

ingredients:
2 1/2 tsp. yeast
1 tsp. salt
3 1/2 cups bread flour
3 tbsp. sugar
1/2 cup egg substitute
1 egg white
1 1/3 cups nonfat sour cream

directions:
Add ingredients in the order suggested by the bread machine manufacturer and follow baking instructions provided in the manual.

Nutrition per Serving	1-Pound	1 1/2-Pound
Calories	163	156
Carbohydrate	29 grams	27 grams
Cholesterol	0 milligrams	0 milligrams
Dietary Fiber	2 grams	2 grams
Protein	7 grams	7 grams
Sodium	233 milligrams	216 milligrams

Exchanges

	2 starch	2 starch

WHOLESOME FRUIT BREAD

1 -POUND RECIPE (8 SLICES)

ingredients:
1 1/2 tsp. yeast
3/4 tsp. salt
1 tbsp. sugar
1 tbsp. nonfat dry milk powder
2 cups bread flour
1 tbsp. lite applesauce
3/4 cup water
1/2 cup dried mixed fruit

1 1/2-POUND RECIPE (12 SLICES)

ingredients:
2 tsp. yeast
1 tsp. salt
1 1/2 tbsp. sugar
2 tbsp. nonfat dry milk powder
3 cups bread flour
2 tbsp. lite applesauce
1 1/4 cups water
1 cup dried mixed fruit

directions:
Add ingredients in the order suggested by the bread machine manufacturer and follow baking instructions provided in the manual.

Nutrition per Serving	1-Pound	1 1/2-Pound
Calories	136	144
Carbohydrate	28 grams	31 grams
Cholesterol	<1 milligram	<1 milligram
Protein	4 grams	4 grams
Dietary Fiber	2 grams	2 grams
Sodium	206 milligrams	185 milligrams

Exchanges

	1-Pound	1 1/2-Pound
	1 1/3 starch	1 1/3 starch
	2/3 fruit	2/3 fruit

WHOLE WHEAT APPLE-OATMEAL BREAD

1-POUND RECIPE (8 SLICES)

ingredients: 1 tsp. yeast
3/4 tsp. salt
1 tbsp. nonfat dry milk powder
3/4 tsp. cinnamon
1/4 cup multi-grain oatmeal
2 1/4 cups whole wheat flour
1 tbsp. apple butter
1/4 cup frozen apple juice concentrate, thawed
1/2 tbsp. corn syrup
1 cup + 3 tbsp. water

1 1/2-POUND RECIPE (12 SLICES)

ingredients: 1 1/2 tsp. yeast
1 1/2 tsp. salt
2 tbsp. nonfat dry milk powder
1 1/2 tsp. cinnamon
1/3 cup multi-grain oatmeal
3 1/4 cups whole wheat flour
2 tbsp. apple butter
1/3 cup frozen apple juice concentrate, thawed
1 tbsp. corn syrup
1 1/4 cups water

directions: Add ingredients in the order suggested by the bread machine manufacturer and follow baking instructions provided in the manual.

Nutrition per Serving	1-Pound	1 1/2-Pound
Calories	150	147
Carbohydrate	33 grams	32 grams
Cholesterol	<1 milligram	<1 milligram
Dietary Fiber	5 grams	5 grams
Protein	6 grams	5 grams
Sodium	208 milligrams	276 milligrams
Exchanges	2 starch	2 starch

WHOLE WHEAT APPLE-RAISIN BREAD

1-POUND RECIPE (8 SLICES)

ingredients:
1 tsp. yeast
3/4 tsp. salt
3/4 tsp. cinnamon
1 cup bread flour
1 1/4 cups whole wheat flour
1 tbsp. nonfat dry milk powder
1 tbsp. frozen apple juice concentrate, thawed
1/4 cup lite applesauce
3/4 cup + 1 tbsp. water
1/4 cup raisins

1 1/2-POUND RECIPE (12 SLICES)

ingredients:
1 1/2 tsp. yeast
1 1/4 tsp. salt
1 1/2 tsp. cinnamon
1 1/2 cups bread flour
1 3/4 cups whole wheat flour
2 tbsp. nonfat dry milk powder
2 tbsp. sugar
2 tbsp. frozen apple juice concentrate, thawed
1/3 cup lite applesauce
1 cup water
1/3 cup raisins

directions:
Add ingredients in the order suggested by the bread machine manufacturer and follow baking instructions provided in the manual.

Nutrition per Serving	1-Pound	1 1/2-Pound
Calories	145	143
Carbohydrate	31 grams	31 grams
Cholesterol	<1 milligram	<1 milligram
Dietary Fiber	4 grams	3 grams
Protein	5 grams	5 grams
Sodium	206 milligrams	230 milligrams

Exchanges		
	1 2/3 starch	1 2/3 starch
	1/3 fruit	1/3 fruit

WHOLE WHEAT BREAD

1-POUND RECIPE (8 SLICES)

ingredients: 1 1/2 tsp. yeast
1 tsp. gluten
1/4 cup nonfat dry milk powder
1 1/2 cups bread flour
1 1/2 cups whole wheat flour
2 tbsp. molasses
2 tbsp. Lighter Bake
1 cup water

1 1/2-POUND RECIPE (12 SLICES)

ingredients: 2 1/2 tsp. yeast
2 tsp. gluten
1/3 cup nonfat dry milk powder
1 3/4 cups bread flour
1 3/4 cups whole wheat flour
3 tbsp. molasses
3 tbsp. Lighter Bake
1 1/3 cups water

directions: Add ingredients in the order suggested by the bread machine manufacturer and follow baking instructions provided in the manual.

Nutrition per Serving	1-Pound	1 1/2-Pound
Calories	184	150
Carbohydrate	38 grams	31 grams
Cholesterol	<1 milligram	<1 milligram
Dietary Fiber	4 grams	3 grams
Protein	7 grams	6 grams
Sodium	19 milligrams	15 milligrams

Exchanges

	1-Pound	1 1/2-Pound
	2 starch	2 starch
	1/2 fruit	

WHOLE WHEAT DINNER ROLLS

ingredients:

1-POUND RECIPE (12 ROLLS)
1 1/2 tsp. yeast
1/2 tsp. salt
1 1/3 cups bread flour
1/3 cup whole wheat flour
1/4 cup egg substitute
1 1/2 tbsp. lite applesauce
1 1/2 tbsp. honey
1/2 cup water

ingredients:

1 1/2-POUND RECIPE (18 ROLLS)
2 tsp. yeast
3/4 tsp. salt
2 cups bread flour
1 cup whole wheat flour
1/4 cup egg substitute
2 tbsp. lite applesauce
2 tbsp. honey
3/4 cup water

directions:

Add ingredients in order suggested by bread machine manufacturer and process on dough cycle. Remove from machine; place on floured surface. Gently stretch dough; roll into long rope. Lightly spray muffin tins with nonfat cooking spray. Divide dough into equal pieces; place in muffin tin. Cover; let rise in warm place 30 minutes, until doubled in size. Preheat oven to 400 degrees. Bake 12 to 15 minutes, until lightly browned.

Nutrition per Serving	1-Pound	1 1/2-Pound
Calories	69	79
Carbohydrate	14 grams	16 grams
Cholesterol	0 milligrams	0 milligrams
Dietary Fiber	1 gram	1 gram
Protein	3 grams	3 grams
Sodium	97 milligrams	95 milligrams
Exchanges	1 starch	1 starch

WHOLE WHEAT OATMEAL BREAD

1-POUND RECIPE (8 SLICES)

ingredients:
1 tsp. yeast
3/4 tsp. salt
2 1/4 cups whole wheat flour
1/4 cup multi-grain oatmeal
1 tbsp. lite applesauce
1 cup skim milk
1/2 cup water

1 1/2-POUND RECIPE (12 SLICES)

ingredients:
1 1/2 tsp. yeast
1 1/2 tsp. salt
3 1/4 cups whole wheat flour
1/3 cup multi-grain oatmeal
2 tbsp. lite applesauce
1 1/4 cups skim milk
1/2 cup water

directions:
Add ingredients in the order suggested by the bread machine manufacturer and follow baking instructions provided in the manual.

Nutrition per Serving	1-Pound	1 1/2-Pound
Calories	137	130
Carbohydrate	28 grams	28 grams
Cholesterol	<1 milligram	<1 milligram
Dietary Fiber	5 grams	5 grams
Protein	6 grams	6 grams
Sodium	218 milligrams	282 milligrams

Exchanges

	1 2/3 starch	1 2/3 starch

WHOLE WHEAT RAISIN BREAD

1-POUND RECIPE (8 SLICES)

ingredients:
1 tsp. yeast
3/4 tsp. salt
3/4 tsp. cinnamon
1 cup bread flour
1 1/4 cups whole wheat flour
1 tbsp. nonfat dry milk powder
1 tbsp. sugar
1 tbsp. frozen apple juice concentrate, thawed
1/4 cup lite applesauce
3/4 cup + 1 tbsp. water
1/4 cup raisins

1 1/2-POUND RECIPE (12 SLICES)

ingredients:
1 1/2 tsp. yeast
1 1/4 tsp. salt
1 1/2 tsp. cinnamon
1 1/2 cups bread flour
1 3/4 cups whole wheat flour
2 tbsp. nonfat dry milk powder
2 tbsp. sugar
2 tbsp. frozen apple juice concentrate, thawed
1/3 cup lite applesauce
1 cup water
1/3 cup raisins

directions:
Add ingredients in the order suggested by the bread machine manufacturer and follow baking instructions provided in the manual.

Nutrition per Serving	1-Pound	1 1/2-Pound
Calories	145	143
Carbohydrate	31 grams	31 grams
Cholesterol	<1 milligram	<1 milligram
Dietary Fiber	4 grams	3 grams
Protein	5 grams	5 grams
Sodium	206 milligrams	230 milligrams
Exchanges	1 2/3 starch	1 2/3 starch
	1/3 fruit	1/3 fruit

WHOLE WHEAT
SOURDOUGH BREAD

1-POUND RECIPE (8 SLICES)

ingredients:
1 tsp. yeast
1/2 tsp. salt
1/2 cup bread flour
1 1/3 cups whole-grain wheat flour
1/2 cup sourdough starter
1 1/2 tbsp. sugar
5/8 cup water

1 1/2-POUND RECIPE (12 SLICES)

ingredients:
1 1/2 tsp. yeast
3/4 tsp. salt
1 cup bread flour
2 cups whole-grain wheat flour
3/4 cup sourdough starter
2 tbsp. sugar
1 cup water

directions:
Add ingredients in the order suggested by the bread machine manufacturer and follow baking instructions provided in the manual.

Nutrition per Serving	1-Pound	1 1/2-Pound
Calories	109	116
Carbohydrate	23 grams	25 grams
Cholesterol	<1 milligram	<1 milligram
Dietary Fiber	3 grams	3 grams
Protein	4 grams	4 grams
Sodium	136 milligrams	136 milligrams

Exchanges

	1 1/3 starch	1 1/3 starch
	1/3 fruit	1/3 fruit

YOGURT BREAD

1-POUND RECIPE (8 SLICES)

ingredients:
1 tsp. yeast
3/4 tsp. salt
1 tbsp. nonfat dry milk powder
1 tbsp. sugar
2 1/4 cups bread flour
1 tbsp. lite applesauce
1 tbsp. sesame seeds
1/2 cup nonfat yogurt
1/2 cup water

1 1/2-POUND RECIPE (12 SLICES)

ingredients:
1 1/2 tsp. yeast
1 1/4 tsp. salt
2 tbsp. nonfat dry milk powder
2 tbsp. sugar
3 1/4 cups bread flour
2 tbsp. lite applesauce
2 tbsp. sesame seeds
3/4 cup nonfat yogurt
3/4 cup water

directions: Add ingredients in the order suggested by the bread machine manufacturer and follow baking instructions provided in the manual.

Nutrition per Serving	1-Pound	1 1/2-Pound
Calories	138	139
Carbohydrate	26 grams	26 grams
Cholesterol	<1 milligram	<1 milligram
Dietary Fiber	2 grams	2 grams
Protein	5 grams	5 grams
Sodium	216 milligrams	240 milligrams

Exchanges

	1 2/3 starch	1 2/3 starch

YUMMY STICKY BUNS

ingredients: **1-POUND RECIPE (12 STICKY BUNS)**
1-Pound Sweet Dough Recipe
1/4 cup corn syrup
3/4 cup brown sugar, divided
2 1/2 tbsp. melted fat-free margarine, divided
1 tsp. cinnamon
2 tbsp. raisins
2 tbsp. chopped dates

ingredients: **1 1/2-POUND RECIPE (18 STICKY BUNS)**
1 1/2-Pound Sweet Dough Recipe
5 tbsp. corn syrup
1 cup + 1 tbsp. brown sugar, divided
3 tbsp. melted fat-free margarine, divided
1 1/2 tsp. cinnamon
3 tbsp. raisins
2 tbsp. chopped dates

directions: Prepare Sweet Dough Recipe according to directions. Turn dough on lightly-floured surface; shape into log. Lightly spray 9x13-inch baking dish (1 1/2-Pound Recipe) or 9-inch cake pan (1-Pound Recipe) with nonfat cooking spray. Sprinkle 1/2 to 3/4 cup brown sugar in bottom of prepared pan; top with corn syrup; blend lightly.

Roll dough into large rectangle. Brush dough with 1 tablespoon fat-free margarine; sprinkle with remaining brown sugar, cinnamon, raisins and dates. Roll dough up lengthwise; seal ends. Slice in equal pieces; place in prepared pan. Brush tops of rolls with remaining melted margarine. Cover with plastic wrap (lightly sprayed with nonfat cooking spray); let rise in warm place 30 to 45 minutes, until doubled in size. Preheat oven to 325 degrees. Bake rolls in preheated oven 40 to 45 minutes, until lightly browned. Remove from oven; invert rolls onto large platter. Serve immediately.

Nutrition per Serving	1-Pound	1 1/2-Pound
Calories	190	182
Carbohydrate	43 grams	41 grams
Cholesterol	<1 milligram	<1 milligram
Dietary Fiber	1 gram	1 gram
Protein	4 grams	4 grams
Sodium	**150 milligrams**	**145 milligrams**
Exchanges	1 1/3 starch	1 1/3 starch
	1 1/2 fruit	1 1/3 fruit

ZUCCHINI BREAD

1-POUND RECIPE (8 SLICES)

ingredients:
1 tsp. yeast
1 tsp. salt
1 tbsp. sugar
1 tbsp. nonfat dry milk powder
2 3/4 cups bread flour
2 tsp. cinnamon
1/4 cup grated zucchini
1 tbsp. Lighter Bake
1 cup water

1 1/2-POUND RECIPE (12 SLICES)

ingredients:
1 1/2 tsp. yeast
1 1/2 tsp. salt
1 1/2 tbsp. sugar
2 tbsp. nonfat dry milk powder
3 1/4 cups bread flour
2 1/2 tsp. cinnamon
1/3 cup grated zucchini
2 tbsp. Lighter Bake
1 1/3 cups water

directions:
Add ingredients in the order suggested by the bread machine manufacturer and follow baking instructions provided in the manual.

Nutrition per Serving	1-Pound	1 1/2-Pound
Calories	154	127
Carbohydrate	31 grams	26 grams
Cholesterol	<1 milligram	<1 milligram
Dietary Fiber	2 grams	2 grams
Protein	5 grams	4 grams
Sodium	**274 milligrams**	**274 milligrams**

Exchanges

	1-Pound	1 1/2-Pound
	1 2/3 starch	1 1/3 starch
	1/3 fruit	1/3 fruit

ZUCCHINI-CARROT BREAD

1-POUND RECIPE (12 SLICES)

ingredients: 1 1/2 tsp. yeast
3/4 tsp. salt
1 1/2 tsp. cinnamon
1 tbsp. nonfat dry milk powder
1 tbsp. brown sugar
2 cups bread flour
1 tbsp. Lighter Bake
1/2 cup water
1/4 cup grated zucchini
1/4 cup grated carrots

1 1/2-POUND RECIPE (12 SLICES)

ingredients: 1 1/2 tsp. yeast
1 tsp. salt
2 tsp. cinnamon
1 1/2 tbsp. nonfat dry milk powder
1 1/2 tbsp. brown sugar
3 cups bread flour
1 1/2 tbsp. Lighter Bake
3/4 cup water
1/3 cup grated zucchini
1/3 cup grated carrots

directions: Add ingredients in the order suggested by the bread machine manufacturer and follow baking instructions provided in the manual.

Nutrition per Serving	1-Pound	1 1/2-Pound
Calories	120	118
Carbohydrate	24 grams	24 grams
Cholesterol	<1 milligram	<1 milligram
Dietary Fiber	2 grams	2 grams
Protein	4 grams	4 grams
Sodium	208 milligrams	185 milligrams

Exchanges

	1-Pound	1 1/2-Pound
	1 1/3 starch	1 1/3 starch
	1/2 vegetable	1/2 vegetable

ZUCCHINI GINGER BREAD

1-POUND RECIPE (8 SLICES)

ingredients:
1 tsp. yeast
1/4 tsp. salt
3/4 tsp. cinnamon
1 1/4 tsp. ground ginger
2 tbsp. nonfat dry milk powder
1/2 cup whole wheat flour
1 3/4 cups bread flour
1 tsp. apple butter
1 1/2 tbsp. lite applesauce
1/3 cup grated zucchini
3/4 cup water

1 1/2-POUND RECIPE (12 SLICES)

ingredients:
1 1/2 tsp. yeast
1/2 tsp. salt
1 tsp. cinnamon
2 tsp. ground ginger
3 tbsp. nonfat dry milk powder
3/4 cup whole wheat flour
2 2/3 cups bread flour
1 1/2 tsp. apple butter
2 tbsp. lite applesauce
1/2 cup grated zucchini
1 cup water

directions:
Add ingredients in the order suggested by the bread machine manufacturer and follow baking instructions provided in the manual.

Nutrition per Serving	1-Pound	1 1/2-Pound
Calories	126	125
Carbohydrate	25 grams	25 grams
Cholesterol	<1 milligram	<1 milligram
Dietary Fiber	2 grams	2 grams
Protein	5 grams	5 grams
Sodium	75 milligrams	75 milligrams

Exchanges

	1 2/3 starch	1 2/3 starch

BOUNTIFUL
BAGELS

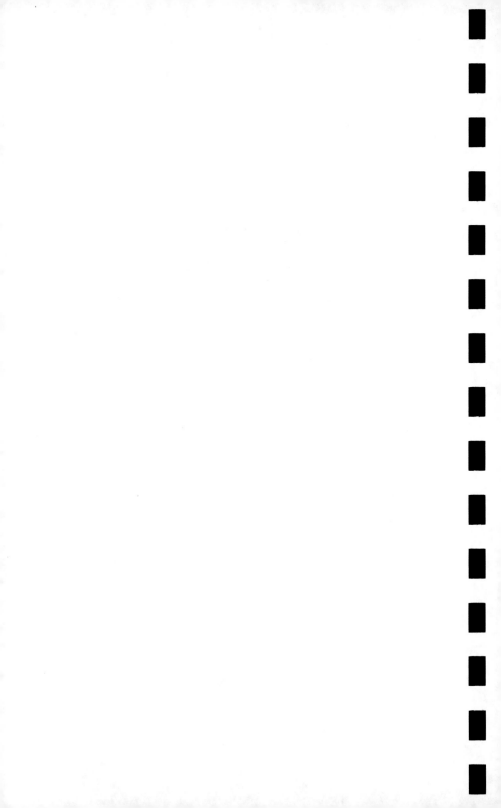

Basic Bagel Baking Instructions

1. Add ingredients in the order suggested by the bread machine manufacturer and process on the dough cycle. Raisins and other dried fruits can be added at the beginning, or kneaded into the dough after the first rise period. Some machines indicate when fruits should be added; the results from testing were the same when fruits were added at the beginning, before the end of the kneading cycle, or after the dough was removed from the machine.

2. Lightly spray baking sheets with nonfat cooking spray.

3. Remove dough from the machine and place on a lightly-floured surface. Punch dough down and knead several times to remove any air pockets. Let dough rest 5 to 10 minutes.

4. Divide dough into equal pieces (8 - 12) and roll each piece into a ball. Poke your finger (lightly floured) through the center; stretch and smooth dough to form a hole in the center. Dough can also be shaped into 6-inch logs for bagel sticks. Place on prepared baking sheets. Cover with plastic wrap and let rise in a warm place until puffy, about 20 - 30 minutes.

5. Fill a large soup pot or Dutch oven with 3 - 4 inches of water. Heat over high heat to boiling.

6. Preheat oven to 400 degrees.

7. Carefully drop bagels into boiling water. Drop 4 - 5 bagels at a time so they are barely touching. Bagels will expand in water so do not crowd in the pot. Reduce temperature to medium-low and boil bagels 30 seconds to 1 minute on each side. Flip bagels carefully by using a large, slotted spoon or spatula. Remove bagels and place on lightly-floured towel to drain. Place on baking sheets. Some bagel recipes do not require boiling; proceed to step 8.

8. If desired, brush bagels with warm water, spray with nonfat cooking spray, or brush with egg wash (1/4 cup egg substitute or 1 egg white mixed with 1 - 2 tablespoons water or skim milk). Sprinkle tops with salt, seeds, onions, garlic, assorted herbs or any combination, if desired.

9. Bake immediately in preheated oven 20-25 minutes, until lightly browned.

10. Store bagels in the freezer if not using immediately. Defrost in the microwave 30 seconds on medium heat, or 15 - 20 minutes at room temperature. For easy serving, slice bagels before freezing and toast bagel halves directly from the freezer.

Special Hints for Best Bagels:

1. Use warm water (105 - 115 degrees F) to activate yeast.

2. If the dough is wet and sticky, add flour 1 tablespoon at a time until dough forms a ball.

3. If the dough is too dry and crumbly, add water 1 tablespoon at a time until dough forms a ball.

4. Bagels bake the best on a darker surface; try to avoid using shiny aluminum for baking. If bagels still burn on the bottom, reduce the oven temperature and increase baking time until bagels are lightly browned.

5. Make sure to use fresh yeast that has been storeed in the refrigerator. Expired yeast can affect the rising of the dough.

APPLE-RAISIN BAGELS

1-POUND RECIPE (8 BAGELS)

ingredients:
1 1/2 tsp. yeast
1/2 tsp. salt
1 tbsp. sugar
1 1/2 tsp. cinnamon
2 1/4 cups bread flour
1/2 cup + 1 tbsp. apple butter
3/4 cup water
1/2 cup raisins

1 1/2-POUND RECIPE (12 BAGELS)

ingredients:
2 1/2 tsp. yeast
3/4 tsp. salt
2 tbsp. sugar
2 tsp. cinnamon
3 cups + 3 tbsp. bread flour
1 cup apple butter
1 cup water
3/4 cup raisins

directions: Follow basic bagel baking instructions.

Nutrition per Serving	1-Pound	1 1/2-Pound
Calories	217	196
Carbohydrate	47 grams	43 grams
Cholesterol	0 milligrams	0 milligrams
Dietary Fiber	2 grams	2 grams
Protein	5 grams	5 grams
Sodium	138 milligrams	137 milligrams

Exchanges

	2 starch	1 2/3 starch
	1 fruit	1 fruit

BAGEL CHIPS

ingredients: Assorted bagels
Dried herbs, seeds, onion powder,
garlic powder, cinnamon-sugar or
combination

directions: Preheat oven to 350 degrees. Lightly spray baking
sheet with nonfat cooking spray. Slice bagels (day-
old bagels are best) horizontally into thin slices
and place on prepared sheet. Lightly spray with
nonfat cooking spray and sprinkle with desired
toppings. Bake in preheated oven 10 to 15 minutes,
until lightly browned and crisp.
Great with dips, flavored cream cheese or spreads.

Nutrition per Serving*

*Analysis varies with each bagel. You may use the
nutrition per serving for each individual bagel.

BAGEL DOGS

ingredients: 1 1/2 -Pound Water Bagel Recipe
8 fat-free hot dogs

directions: Add Water Bagel recipe ingredients in the order suggested by the bread machine manufacturer and process on the dough cycle. Divide dough into 8 equal pieces; roll each piece into a rectangle. Place hot dog in the center of dough; seal dough around the hot dog.
Preheat oven to 350 degrees. Lightly spray baking sheet with nonfat cooking spray. Place bagel dogs on baking sheet and bake in preheated oven 20 to 25 minutes, until bagel is lightly browned on all sides. Rotate bagel dogs halfway through cooking time.

Serves 8.

Nutrition per Serving
Calories	237
Carbohydrate	42 grams
Cholesterol	15 milligrams
Dietary Fiber	2 grams
Protein	13 grams
Sodium	694 milligrams

Exchanges
1 2/3 meat
2 2/3 starch

BLUEBERRY BAGELS

1-POUND RECIPE (8 BAGELS)

ingredients: 1 1/2 tsp. yeast
3/4 tsp. salt
1 tbsp. sugar
2 1/2 cups bread flour
1 cup + 1 tbsp. water
1/2 cup dried blueberries

1 1/2-POUND RECIPE (12 BAGELS)

ingredients: 2 1/2 tsp. yeast
1 tsp. salt
2 tbsp. sugar
3 1/3 cups bread flour
1 cup water + 3 tbsp. water
3/4 cup dried blueberries

directions: Follow basic bagel baking instructions.

Nutrition per Serving	1-Pound	1 1/2-Pound
Calories	140	128
Carbohydrate	28 grams	26 grams
Cholesterol	0 milligrams	0 milligrams
Dietary Fiber	2 grams	2 grams
Protein	5 grams	4 grams
Sodium	203 milligrams	181 milligrams

Exchanges

	1-Pound	1 1/2-Pound
	1 2/3 starch	1 1/3 starch
	1/3 fruit	1/3 fruit

CARROT-ZUCCHINI BAGELS

1-POUND RECIPE (8 BAGELS)

ingredients:
1 1/2 tsp. yeast
1/2 tsp. salt
1/2 tsp. cinnamon
1 tbsp. brown sugar
2 3/4 cups bread flour
1 1/2 tbsp. Lighter Bake
1/4 cup egg substitute
1/4 cup grated carrots
1/4 cup grated zucchini
1/2 cup water

1 1/2-POUND RECIPE (12 BAGELS)

ingredients:
2 1/2 tsp. yeast
3/4 tsp. salt
3/4 tsp. cinnamon
2 tbsp. brown sugar
3 3/4 cups bread flour
2 tbsp. Lighter Bake
1/4 cup egg substitute
1/2 cup grated carrots
1/2 cup grated zucchini
3/4 cup water

directions: Add ingredients in order suggested by bread machine manufacturer and process on dough cycle. Remove dough from machine; follow basic instructions for the second rise. Do not boil bagels; bake immediately after second rise. Preheat oven to 350 degrees; bake 20 to 25 minutes, until lightly browned.

Nutrition per Serving	1-Pound	1 1/2-Pound
Calories	160	149
Carbohydrate	32 grams	30 grams
Cholesterol	0 milligrams	0 milligrams
Dietary Fiber	2 grams	2 grams
Protein	6 grams	5 grams
Sodium	149 milligrams	146 milligrams

Exchanges

	2 starch	2 starch

CINNAMON-RAISIN BAGELS

1-POUND RECIPE (8 BAGELS)

ingredients:
1 1/2 tsp. yeast
1/2 tsp. salt
1 tbsp. sugar
1 1/2 tsp. cinnamon
2 3/4 cups bread flour
3/4 cup + 1 tbsp. water
1/2 cup raisins

1 1/2-POUND RECIPE (12 BAGELS)

ingredients:
2 tsp. yeast
3/4 tsp. salt
2 tbsp. sugar
2 tsp. cinnamon
3 1/3 cups bread flour
1 3/8 cups water
3/4 cup raisins

directions: Follow basic bagel baking instructions

Nutrition per Serving	1-Pound	1 1/2-Pound
Calories	176	150
Carbohydrate	37 grams	32 grams
Cholesterol	0 milligrams	0 milligrams
Dietary Fiber	2 grams	2 grams
Protein	5 grams	5 grams
Sodium	138 milligrams	137 milligrams

Exchanges

	1 2/3 starch	1 2/3 starch
	2/3 fruit	1/2 fruit

CRAISIN-RAISIN BAGELS

ingredients:

1-POUND RECIPE (8 BAGELS)
1 1/2 tsp. yeast
1/2 tsp. salt
2 3/4 cups bread flour
1 tbsp. honey
3/4 cup + 1 tbsp. water
1/4 cup craisins
1/4 cup raisins

ingredients:

1 1/2-POUND RECIPE (12 BAGELS)
2 tsp. yeast
3/4 tsp. salt
3 1/3 cups bread flour
2 tbsp. honey
1 cup + 3 tbsp. water
1/2 cup craisins
1/4 cup golden raisins

directions: Follow basic bagel baking instructions.

Nutrition per Serving	1-Pound	1 1/2-Pound
Calories	177	152
Carbohydrate	37 grams	32 grams
Cholesterol	0 milligrams	0 milligrams
Dietary Fiber	2 grams	2 grams
Protein	5 grams	4 grams
Sodium	137 milligrams	136 milligrams

Exchanges

	1-Pound	1 1/2-Pound
	1 1/3 starch	1 2/3 starch
	3/4 fruit	3/4 fruit

141

CRUNCHY DATE BAGELS

1-POUND RECIPE (8 BAGELS)

ingredients: 1 1/2 tsp. yeast
1/2 tsp. salt
1 tbsp. sugar
2 3/4 cups bread flour
1/2 cup Grape-Nuts
3/4 cup + 1 tbsp. water
1/2 cup chopped dates

1 1/2-POUND RECIPE (12 BAGELS)

ingredients: 2 tsp. yeast
3/4 tsp. salt
2 tbsp. sugar
3 1/3 cups bread flour
3/4 cup Grape-Nuts
1 cup + 3 tbsp. water
3/4 cup chopped dates

directions: Follow basic bagel baking instructions.

Nutrition per Serving	1-Pound	1 1/2-Pound
Calories	203	170
Carbohydrate	43 grams	39 grams
Cholesterol	0 milligrams	0 milligrams
Dietary Fiber	3 grams	3 grams
Protein	6 grams	5 grams
Sodium	186 milligrams	186 milligrams

Exchanges

	2 starch	1 2/3 starch
	3/4 fruit	3/4 fruit

EGG BAGELS

ingredients: **1-POUND RECIPE (8 BAGELS)**
1 1/2 tsp. yeast
1/2 tsp. salt
1 tbsp. sugar
2 1/2 cups bread flour
1 1/2 tbsp. lite applesauce
1/4 cup egg substitute
3/4 cup water

ingredients: **1 1/2-POUND RECIPE (12 BAGELS)**
2 tsp. yeast
3/4 tsp. salt
2 tbsp. sugar
3 1/3 cups bread flour
2 tbsp. lite applesauce
1/4 cup egg substitute
1 cup water

directions: Follow basic bagel baking instructions through second rising period. For softer bagel, do not boil bagels before baking.

Nutrition per Serving	1-Pound	1 1/2-Pound
Calories	139	125
Carbohydrate	27 grams	25 grams
Cholesterol	0 milligrams	0 milligrams
Dietary Fiber	2 grams	2 grams
Protein	5 grams	5 grams
Sodium	146 milligrams	143 milligrams

Exchanges

	1 2/3 starch	1 2/3 starch

FRUIT BAGELS

1-POUND RECIPE (8 BAGELS)

ingredients:
1 1/2 tsp. yeast
3/4 tsp. salt
1 tbsp. brown sugar
1 1/2 tsp. cinnamon
1 tsp. nutmeg
2 3/4 cups bread flour
3/4 cup + 1 tbsp. water
1/2 cup dried mixed fruit

1 1/2-POUND RECIPE (12 BAGELS)

ingredients:
2 1/2 tsp. yeast
1 tsp. salt
2 tbsp. brown sugar
2 tsp. cinnamon
1 1/2 tsp. nutmeg
3 1/3 cups bread flour
1 cup + 3 tbsp. water
3/4 cup dried mixed fruit

directions: Follow basic bagel baking instructions.

Nutrition per Serving	1-Pound	1 1/2-Pound
Calories	178	154
Carbohydrate	37 grams	33 grams
Cholesterol	0 milligrams	0 milligrams
Dietary Fiber	2 grams	2 grams
Protein	5 grams	5 grams
Sodium	209 milligrams	182 milligrams

Exchanges

	1 2/3 starch	1 2/3 starch
	3/4 fruit	1/2 fruit

GRANOLA APPLE BAGELS

1-POUND RECIPE (8 BAGELS)

ingredients:
1 1/2 tsp. yeast
3/4 tsp. salt
1 1/2 tbsp. brown sugar
2 5/8 cups bread flour
3/4 cup lite applesauce
1/2 cup water
1/2 cup dried apples, chopped
1/2 cup nonfat granola

1 1/2-POUND RECIPE (12 BAGELS)

ingredients:
2 1/2 tsp. yeast
1 tsp. salt
2 3/4 tbsp. brown sugar
3 1/2 cups bread flour
1 cup lite applesauce
1 1/4 cups water
3/4 cup dried apples, chopped
1/2 cup nonfat granola

directions: Follow basic bagel baking instructions.

Nutrition per Serving	1-Pound	1 1/2-Pound
Calories	188	166
Carbohydrate	40 grams	36 grams
Cholesterol	3 milligrams	2 milligrams
Dietary Fiber	3 grams	3 grams
Protein	5 grams	5 grams
Sodium	210 milligrams	187 milligrams

Exchanges

	1-Pound	1 1/2-Pound
	1 2/3 starch	1 2/3 starch
	1 fruit	2/3 fruit

OAT BAGELS

1-POUND RECIPE (8 BAGELS)

ingredients:
1 1/2 tsp. yeast
1/2 tsp. salt
1/2 cup rolled oats
2 cups bread flour
1/4 cup whole wheat flour
1 tbsp. brown sugar
3/4 cup + 1 tbsp. water

1 1/2-POUND RECIPE (12 BAGELS)

ingredients:
2 1/2 tsp. yeast
3/4 tsp. salt
1 cup rolled oats
2 cups bread flour
1/2 cup flour, whole-grain wheat
2 tbsp. brown sugar
1 3/8 cups water

directions:
Follow basic bagel baking instructions. Make sure bagels have almost doubled in size during second rising before boiling and baking. If necessary, increase second rising time.

Nutrition per Serving	1-Pound	1 1/2-Pound
Calories	143	123
Carbohydrate	28 grams	24 grams
Cholesterol	0 milligrams	0 milligrams
Dietary Fiber	2 grams	2 grams
Protein	5 grams	5 grams
Sodium	137 milligrams	136 milligrams

Exchanges

	1 2/3 starch	1 2/3 starch

ONION BIALYS

ingredients: **1-POUND RECIPE (8 BIALYS)**
1 1/2 tsp. yeast
1/2 tsp. salt
3 cups bread flour
2 tsp. sugar
3/4 cup water
2 tbsp. minced onions

ingredients: **1 1/2-POUND RECIPE (12 BIALYS)**
2 tsp. yeast
3/4 tsp. salt
3 1/2 cups bread flour
1 tbsp. sugar
1 1/8 cups water
3 tbsp. minced onion

directions: Add ingredients (excluding onions) in the order suggested by the bread machine manufacturer and process on the dough cycle. Remove dough, punch down and let rest 10 minutes. Divide dough into 8 to 12 equal pieces and roll each piece into a 4-inch circle. Lightly spray baking sheet with non-fat cooking spray. Place bialys on sheet, cover with plastic wrap and let rise in a warm place until puffy. Preheat oven to 400 degrees. Make a small indentation in the center of each bialy and spray lightly with nonfat cooking spray; sprinkle minced onions in center. Bake bialys in preheated oven 20-25 minutes, until lightly browned.

Nutrition per Serving	1-Pound	1 1/2-Pound
Calories	159	125
Carbohydrate	32 grams	25 grams
Cholesterol	0 milligrams	0 milligrams
Dietary Fiber	2 grams	2 grams
Protein	6 grams	4 grams
Sodium	137 milligrams	136 milligrams

Exchanges

	1-Pound	1 1/2-Pound
	2 starch	1 2/3 starch

147

ORANGE-BERRY BAGELS

1-POUND RECIPE (8 BAGELS)

ingredients:
1 1/2 tsp. yeast
1/2 tsp. salt
1 tbsp. sugar
2 3/4 cups bread flour
1/2 cup orange juice
1/4 cup water
1/2 cup dried blueberries

1 1/2-POUND RECIPE (12 BAGELS)

ingredients:
2 tsp. yeast
3/4 tsp. salt
2 tbsp. sugar
3 1/3 cups bread flour
1/2 cup + 1 tbsp. orange juice
1/2 cup water
3/4 cup dried blueberries

directions: Follow basic bagel baking instructions.

Nutrition per Serving	1-Pound	1 1/2-Pound
Calories	159	132
Carbohydrate	32 grams	27 grams
Cholesterol	0 milligrams	0 milligrams
Dietary Fiber	2 grams	2 grams
Protein	5 grams	4 grams
Sodium	137 milligrams	137 milligrams

Exchanges

	1-Pound	1 1/2-Pound
	1 2/3 starch	1 1/3 starch
	1/2 fruit	1/2 fruit

POPPY BAGELS

1-POUND RECIPE (8 BAGELS)

ingredients: 1 1/2 tsp. yeast
1/2 tsp. salt
1 tbsp. sugar
1/2 tbsp. poppy seeds
2 3/4 cups bread flour
3/4 cup + 1 tbsp. water

1 1/2-POUND RECIPE (12 BAGELS)

ingredients: 2 tsp. yeast
3/4 tsp. salt
2 tbsp. sugar
1 tbsp. poppy seeds
3 1/3 cups bread flour
1 cup + 3 tbsp. water

directions: Follow basic bagel baking instructions.

Nutrition per Serving	1-Pound	1 1/2-Pound
Calories	148	126
Carbohydrate	29 grams	24 grams
Cholesterol	0 milligrams	0 milligrams
Dietary Fiber	2 grams	2 grams
Protein	5 grams	4 grams
Sodium	137 milligrams	136 milligrams

Exchanges

	1 3/4 starch	1 1/2 starch

PUMPKIN FRUIT BAGELS

1-POUND RECIPE (8 BAGELS)

ingredients: 1 1/2 tsp. yeast
1/2 tsp. salt
1 1/4 tsp. cinnamon
1/2 tsp. nutmeg
1 tbsp. brown sugar
2 3/4 cups bread flour
1/3 cup pumpkin purée
1/2 cup orange juice

1 1/2-POUND RECIPE (12 BAGELS)

ingredients: 2 tsp. yeast
3/4 tsp. salt
1 1/2 tsp. cinnamon
3/4 tsp. nutmeg
2 tbsp. brown sugar
3 1/3 cups bread flour
1/2 cup pumpkin purée
1/2 cup + 1 tbsp. orange juice

directions: Follow basic bagel baking instructions.

Nutrition per Serving	1-Pound	1 1/2-Pound
Calories	160	133
Carbohydrate	32 grams	27 grams
Cholesterol	0 milligrams	0 milligrams
Dietary Fiber	2 grams	2 grams
Protein	5 grams	4 grams
Sodium	138 milligrams	137 milligrams

Exchanges

	1-Pound	1 1/2-Pound
	1 2/3 starch	1 1/3 starch
	1/3 fruit	1/2 fruit

PUMPKIN-SPICE BAGELS

1-POUND RECIPE (8 BAGELS)

ingredients:
1 1/2 tsp. yeast
1/2 tsp. salt
1 tbsp. brown sugar
1 1/2 tsp. cinnamon
3/4 tsp. nutmeg
1/4 tsp. allspice
2 3/4 cups bread flour
1/3 cup pumpkin purée
1/2 cup water
1/2 cup raisins

1 1/2-POUND RECIPE (12 BAGELS)

ingredients:
2 tsp. yeast
3/4 tsp. salt
2 tbsp. brown sugar
2 tsp. cinnamon
1 tsp. nutmeg
1/2 tsp. allspice
3 1/3 cups bread flour
1/2 cup pumpkin purée
1/2 cup + 1 tbsp. water
3/4 cup raisins

directions: Follow basic bagel baking instructions.

Nutrition per Serving	1-Pound	1 1/2-Pound
Calories	181	156
Carbohydrate	38 grams	33 grams
Cholesterol	0 milligrams	0 milligrams
Dietary Fiber	3 grams	2 grams
Protein	6 grams	5 grams
Sodium	139 milligrams	138 milligrams

Exchanges

	1-Pound	1 1/2-Pound
	2 starch	1 2/3 starch
	1/2 fruit	1/2 fruit

RYE BAGELS

1-POUND RECIPE (8 BAGELS)

ingredients: 1 1/2 tsp. yeast
3/4 tsp. salt
1 3/4 cups bread flour
1/2 cup rye flour
1/4 cup cornmeal
3/4 tbsp. unsweetened cocoa powder
1 tbsp. caraway seeds
2 tbsp. honey
1 cup water

1 1/2-POUND RECIPE (12 BAGELS)

ingredients: 2 1/2 tsp. yeast
3/4 tsp. salt
2 1/4 cups bread flour
3/4 cup rye flour
1/3 cup cornmeal
1 tbsp. unsweetened cocoa powder
2 tbsp. caraway seed
3 tbsp. honey
1 1/2 cups water

directions: Follow basic bagel baking instructions. Make sure bagels have almost doubled in size during second rising before boiling and baking. If necessary, increase second rising time.

Nutrition per Serving	1-Pound	1 1/2-Pound
Calories	153	140
Carbohydrate	32 grams	29 grams
Cholesterol	0 milligrams	0 milligrams
Dietary Fiber	2 grams	2 grams
Protein	5 grams	5 grams
Sodium	203 milligrams	136 milligrams

Exchanges

	2 starch	1 2/3 starch

SUN-DRIED TOMATO BAGELS

1-POUND RECIPE (8 BAGELS)

ingredients:
1 1/2 tsp. yeast
1/2 tsp. salt
1 tbsp. molasses
2 cups bread flour
3/4 cup whole wheat flour
3/4 cup + 1 tbsp. water
1/2 cup sun-dried tomatoes

1 1/2-POUND RECIPE (12 BAGELS)

ingredients:
2 1/2 tsp. yeast
3/4 tsp. salt
2 tbsp. molasses
2 cups bread flour
1 1/4 cups whole wheat flour
1 cup + 1 tbsp. water
3/4 cup sun-dried tomatoes

directions: Follow basic bagel baking instructions.

Nutrition per Serving	1-Pound	1 1/2-Pound
Calories	187	160
Carbohydrate	40 grams	35 grams
Cholesterol	0 milligrams	0 milligrams
Dietary Fiber	4 grams	4 grams
Protein	7 grams	6 grams
Sodium	154 milligrams	158 milligrams

Exchanges

	1-Pound	1 1/2-Pound
	2 starch	2 starch
	1 vegetable	1/2 vegetable

SWEET PEACH BAGELS

1-POUND RECIPE (8 BAGELS)

ingredients:
1 1/2 tsp. yeast
1/2 tsp. salt
1 tbsp. sugar
2 3/4 cups bread flour
3/4 cup + 1 tbsp. water
1/2 cup dried peaches

1 1/2-POUND RECIPE (12 BAGELS)

ingredients:
2 tsp. yeast
3/4 tsp. salt
2 tbsp. sugar
3 1/3 cups bread flour
1 cup + 3 tbsp. water
3/4 cup dried peaches

directions: Follow basic bagel baking instructions.

Nutrition per Serving	1-Pound	1 1/2-Pound
Calories	171	146
Carbohydrate	36 grams	31 grams
Cholesterol	0 milligrams	0 milligrams
Dietary Fiber	3 grams	2 grams
Protein	6 grams	5 grams
Sodium	137 milligrams	137 milligrams

Exchanges

	2 starch	1 2/3 starch
	1/3 fruit	1/3 fruit

WATER BAGELS

1-POUND RECIPE (8 BAGELS)

ingredients: 1 1/2 tsp. yeast
1/2 tsp. salt
2 3/4 cups bread flour
1 tbsp. sugar
3/4 cup + 1 tbsp. water

1 1/2-POUND RECIPE (12 BAGELS)

ingredients: 2 tsp. yeast
3/4 tsp. salt
3 1/3 cups bread flour
2 tbsp. sugar
1 cup + 1 tbsp. water

directions: Follow basic bagel baking instructions.

Nutrition per Serving	1-Pound	1 1/2-Pound
Calories	147	122
Carbohydrate	29 grams	25 grams
Cholesterol	0 milligrams	0 milligrams
Dietary Fiber	2 grams	2 grams
Protein	5 grams	4 grams
Sodium	137 milligrams	136 milligrams

Exchanges

	2 starch	1 2/3 starch

WHOLE WHEAT APPLE BAGELS

1-POUND RECIPE (8 BAGELS)

ingredients:
1 1/2 tsp. yeast
3/4 tsp. salt
1 tbsp. sugar
2 cups bread flour
5/8 cup whole wheat flour
3/4 cup lite applesauce
1 tbsp. apple butter
1 medium apple, chopped

1 1/2-POUND RECIPE (12 BAGELS)

ingredients:
2 1/2 tsp. yeast
1 tsp. salt
2 tbsp. sugar
2 3/4 cups bread flour
3/4 cup whole wheat flour
5/8 cup lite applesauce
1 tbsp. apple butter
1 medium apple, chopped

directions: Follow basic bagel instructions.

Nutrition per Serving	1-Pound	1 1/2-Pound
Calories	169	145
Carbohydrate	36 grams	30 grams
Cholesterol	0 milligrams	0 milligrams
Dietary Fiber	4 grams	3 grams
Protein	5 grams	5 grams
Sodium	203 milligrams	181 milligrams

Exchanges

	1-Pound	1 1/2-Pound
	1 2/3 starch	1 2/3 starch
	2/3 fruit	1/3 fruit

WHOLE WHEAT BAGELS

ingredients:
1-POUND RECIPE (8 BAGELS)
1 1/2 tsp. yeast
1/2 tsp. salt
2 cups bread flour
3/4 cup whole wheat flour
1 tbsp. brown sugar
3/4 cup + 1 tbsp. water

ingredients:
1 1/2-POUND RECIPE (12 BAGELS)
2 1/2 tsp. yeast
1 tsp. salt
2 1/3 cups bread flour
1 cup whole wheat flour
2 tbsp. brown sugar
1 cup + 3 tbsp. water

directions: Follow basic bagel baking instructions.

Nutrition per Serving	1-Pound	1 1/2-Pound
Calories	149	125
Carbohydrate	30 grams	26 grams
Cholesterol	0 milligrams	0 milligrams
Dietary Fiber	3 grams	3 grams
Protein	5 grams	5 grams
Sodium	137 milligrams	181 milligrams

Exchanges

	2 starch	1 2/3 starch

WHOLE WHEAT
BANANA BAGELS

1-POUND RECIPE (8 BAGELS)

ingredients: 1 1/2 tsp. yeast
3/4 tsp. salt
1 tbsp. brown sugar
1 cup whole wheat flour
1 1/2 cups bread flour
1/2 cup banana, sliced
1/2 cup + 1 tbsp. water

1 1/2-POUND RECIPE (12 BAGELS)

ingredients: 2 1/2 tsp. yeast
1 tsp. salt
2 tbsp. brown sugar
1 1/4 cups whole wheat flour
2 1/3 cups bread flour
3/4 cup banana, sliced
3/4 cup + 1 tbsp. water

directions: Follow basic bagel baking instructions.

Nutrition per Serving	1-Pound	1 1/2-Pound
Calories	155	140
Carbohydrate	32 grams	29 grams
Cholesterol	0 milligrams	0 milligrams
Dietary Fiber	3 grams	3 grams
Protein	6 grams	5 grams
Sodium	203 milligrams	181 milligrams

Exchanges

	1-Pound	1 1/2-Pound
	1 2/3 starch	1 2/3 starch
	1/3 fruit	1/4 fruit

WHOLE WHEAT BLUEBERRY BAGELS

1-POUND RECIPE (8 BAGELS)

ingredients:
1 1/2 tsp. yeast
3/4 tsp. salt
1 tbsp. brown sugar
3/4 cup whole wheat flour
1 3/4 cups bread flour
3/4 cup + 1 tbsp. water
1/2 cup dried blueberries

1 1/2-POUND RECIPE (12 BAGELS)

ingredients:
2 1/2 tsp. yeast
1 tsp. salt
2 tbsp. brown sugar
1 cup whole wheat flour
2 1/3 cups bread flour
1 cup + 3 tbsp. water
3/4 cup dried blueberries

directions: Follow basic bagel baking instructions.

Nutrition per Serving	1-Pound	1 1/2-Pound
Calories	141	130
Carbohydrate	30 grams	27 grams
Cholesterol	0 milligrams	0 milligrams
Dietary Fiber	3 grams	3 grams
Protein	5 grams	5 grams
Sodium	204 milligrams	181 milligrams

Exchanges

	1 2/3 starch	1 2/3 starch
	1/3 fruit	1/3 fruit

SPECTACULAR
SPREADS

APPLE BUTTER

ingredients: 8 cups peeled, thinly-sliced apples
1/2 cup frozen apple juice, undiluted
1 cup water
1 1/2 tsp. cinnamon
1/4 tsp. nutmeg

directions: Place all the ingredients in a medium saucepan and bring to a boil over medium-high heat. Reduce heat to low and simmer, uncovered, 15 minutes. Remove from heat and cool completely. Place mixture in blender or food processor and purée; refrigerate apple butter.

Serves: 12

Nutrition per Serving
Calories	63
Carbohydrates	16 grams
Cholesterol	0 milligrams
Dietary Fiber	2 grams
Protein	< 1 gram
Sodium	3 milligrams

Exchanges

1 fruit

ARTICHOKE SPREAD

ingredients: 8 1/2 ounce can artichoke hearts (packed in water)
1/2 cup nonfat mayonnaise
1/2 cup nonfat Parmesan cheese

directions: Drain artichokes and mash in medium-size bowl. Add mayonnaise and Parmesan cheese and mix until ingredients are blended. Refrigerate several hours or overnight.

Serves: 8

Nutrition per Serving

Calories	840
Carbohydrate	7 grams
Cholesterol	0 milligrams
Dietary Fiber	0 grams
Protein	3 grams
Sodium	179 milligrams

Exchanges

1 1/2 vegetable

BANANA-BERRY SPREAD

ingredients: 1 cup strawberries
1 large banana
1/4 tsp. cinnamon
1/4 tsp. sugar
1/8 tsp. nutmeg

directions: Mash strawberries and bananas until blended. Add cinnamon, sugar, and nutmeg and mix well. Serve immediately.

Serves: 6

Nutrition per Serving

Calories	26
Carbohydrate	6 grams
Cholesterol	0 milligrams
Dietary Fiber	1 gram
Protein	.3 gram
Sodium	< 1 milligram

Exchanges

1/3 fruit

BANANA SPREAD

ingredients: 2 whole bananas, mashed
4 tbsp. orange juice
1 1/2 tsp. lemon juice
1/2 tsp. nutmeg
1/4 tsp. ginger
1/2 tsp. cinnamon
2 tbsp. raisins

directions: In a small bowl, combine mashed bananas with orange juice, lemon juice and seasonings and mix until blended and smooth. Stir in raisins.

Serves: 6

Nutrition per Serving

Calories	50
Carbohydrate	13 grams
Cholesterol	0 milligrams
Dietary Fiber	1 gram
Protein	< 1 gram
Sodium	< 1 milligram

Exchanges

1 fruit

BEER CHEESE DIP

ingredients:
1 tbsp. low-fat margarine
1/4 cup chopped onion
1 tsp. cornstarch
1/2 tsp. pepper
1 tsp. low-sodium soy sauce
3/4 cup light beer
2 cups nonfat Cheddar cheese, shredded
3 ounces nonfat cream cheese, softened

directions:
Lightly spray medium saucepan with nonfat cooking spray. Melt margarine in saucepan over medium-high heat; add onions and cook until tender and soft, about 5 minutes. Blend in cornstarch, pepper, soy sauce and beer. Cook over medium heat, stirring constantly, until mixture begins to bubble and slightly thickens. Add Cheddar and cream cheese; cook, stirring constantly, until cheeses are melted and mixture is blended smooth.

Serves: 8

Nutrition per Serving

Calories	68
Carbohydrate	4 grams
Cholesterol	0 milligrams
Dietary Fiber	< 1 gram
Protein	9 grams
Sodium	400 milligrams

Exchanges

1 meat
1/3 starch

BERRY-BERRY CHEESE SPREAD

ingredients: 8 ounces nonfat cream cheese, softened
4 tsp. nonfat sour cream
2 tbsp. fresh blueberries
2 tbsp. fresh raspberries

directions: In a small bowl, mash blueberries and raspberries with a fork. Combine mashed berries, cream cheese, and sour cream in blender or food processor and purée until smooth; refrigerate.

Serves: 8

Nutrition per Serving

Calories	25
Carbohydrate	2 grams
Cholesterol	0 milligrams
Dietary Fiber	< 1 gram
Protein	4 grams
Sodium	179 milligrams

Exchanges

2/3 lean meat

BLACK BEAN SPREAD

ingredients: 8 ounces nonfat cream cheese, softened
8 ounces canned black beans, drained and mashed
3/4 tsp. onion powder
3/4 tsp. minced garlic

directions: Place all ingredients in food processor or blender and process until mixture is smooth. Cover and chill 2 to 3 hours before serving.

Serves: 8

Nutrition per Serving
Calories	60
Carbohydrate	9 grams
Cholesterol	0 milligrams
Dietary Fiber	1 gram
Protein	6 grams
Sodium	177 milligrams

Exchanges
1/2 starch
1/2 meat

CHEDDAR-GARLIC CHEESE SPREAD

ingredients: 8 ounces nonfat cream cheese
8 ounces nonfat shredded Cheddar cheese
1 tsp. minced garlic
2 tbsp. paprika

directions: Soften Cheddar and cream cheese; add minced garlic. Cream mixture and shape into a ball. Sprinkle with paprika. Cover cheese spread with plastic wrap and refrigerate several hours before serving.

Serves: 8

Nutrition per Serving

Calories	69
Carbohydrate	5 grams
Cholesterol	0 milligrams
Dietary Fiber	0 milligrams
Protein	11 grams
Sodium	442 milligrams

Exchanges

1 1/2 meat
1/3 starch

CHEESE-CORN SPREAD

ingredients: 6 ounces nonfat cream cheese, softened
2 tbsp. nonfat sour cream
2 tbsp. skim milk
1/2 cup nonfat Cheddar cheese, shredded
1/2 cup whole kernel corn, drained
1/2 tsp. onion powder
1 1/2 tsp. chili power

directions: Combine cream cheese, sour cream, and milk and mix until blended smooth. Stir in cheese, corn and seasonings until mixed. Refrigerate several hours or overnight.

Serves: 8

Nutrition per Serving

Calories	41
Carbohydrate	5 grams
Cholesterol	4 milligrams
Dietary Fiber	.3 gram
Protein	5 grams
Sodium	213 milligrams

Exchanges

1/3 starch
1/2 meat

CHEESE-ONION SPREAD

ingredients: 8 ounces nonfat cream cheese, softened
1/2 cup nonfat mayonnaise
3 tsp. green onions, sliced
1/2 tsp. onion powder

directions: Combine all ingredients and mix until smooth. Store in refrigerator.

Serves: 6

Nutrition per Serving
Calories   42
Carbohydrate   5 grams
Cholesterol   0 milligrams
Dietary Fiber   0 grams
Protein   5 grams
Sodium   376 milligrams

Exchanges
1/3 starch
1/2 meat

CINNAMON-RAISIN SPREAD

ingredients:　　8 ounces nonfat cream cheese, softened
　　　　　　　　　1 1/2 tsp. cinnamon
　　　　　　　　　1/2 tsp. sugar
　　　　　　　　　1/4 cup golden raisins

directions:　　Combine cream cheese, cinnamon and sugar in food processor or blender, and process until smooth. Fold in raisins; refrigerate.

Serves: 6

Nutrition per Serving

Calories	49
Carbohydrate	8 grams
Cholesterol	0 milligrams
Dietary Fiber	.3 gram
Protein	5 grams
Sodium	237 milligrams

Exchanges

　　　　　　　　1/2 fruit
　　　　　　　　2/3 meat

COTTAGE CHEESE SPREAD

ingredients: 1 lb. nonfat cottage cheese
1 tbsp. chopped chives
1/4 cup chopped cucumber
1/2 cup chopped red and green bell pepper
1/4 tsp. onion powder
1/2 tsp. garlic powder
1 tbsp. paprika

directions: Combine all ingredients in a small bowl and mix
well. Refrigerate at least one hour before serving.
Great with bagel chips!

Serves: 4

Nutrition per Serving

Calories	83
Carbohydrate	6 grams
Cholesterol	9 milligrams
Dietary Fiber	< 1 gram
Protein	14 grams
Sodium	345 milligrams

Exchanges

1 vegetable
1 2/3 meat

CREAMY TUNA SPREAD

ingredients: 6 ounces nonfat cream cheese, softened
6 ounces low-fat tuna in water, drained
3 tbsp. nonfat mayonnaise
1 tbsp. lemon juice
1/2 tsp. onion powder
1/4 tsp. garlic powder

directions: In a medium bowl, combine softened cream cheese and drained tuna and mash until mixed. Add mayonnaise, lemon juice and seasonings, and mix until ingredients are blended. Refrigerate several hours before serving.

Serves: 4

Nutrition per Serving

Calories	97
Carbohydrate	5 grams
Cholesterol	8 milligrams
Dietary Fiber	< 1 gram
Protein	18 grams
Sodium	496 milligrams

Exchanges

2 1/2 meat
1/3 starch

CRUNCHY APPLE CHEESE SPREAD

ingredients: 8 ounces nonfat cream cheese, softened
4 tsp. skim milk
1 cup nonfat shredded Cheddar cheese
1/3 cup Grape-Nuts
3/4 tbsp. sugar
1/2 tsp. cinnamon
1/4 cup chopped apple

directions: Combine cream cheese, milk, cheese, Grape-Nuts, sugar and cinnamon in a food processor or blender, and process until smooth. Fold in apple; refrigerate.

Serves: 8

Nutrition per Serving

Calories	68
Carbohydrate	9 grams
Cholesterol	0 milligrams
Dietary Fiber	< 1 gram
Protein	8 grams
Sodium	352 milligrams

Exchanges

1 meat
1/2 starch

EGG SPREAD

ingredients: 6 whole egg whites, hard-boiled, peeled and diced
2 tbsp. nonfat mayonnaise
1/2 tsp. fat-free Dijon mustard
3/4 tsp. dill
1/2 tbsp. white wine vinegar
1/4 tsp. Worcestershire sauce
1/8 tsp. pepper

directions: Hard-boil eggs, cool, and peel. Discard yolk; dice cooked egg whites. In a medium bowl, combine egg whites with remaining ingredients and chill 1 to 2 hours. Great on pumpernickel bread!

Serves: 4

Nutrition per Serving
Calories	32
Carbohydrate	2 grams
Cholesterol	0 milligrams
Dietary Fiber	< 1 gram
Protein	5 grams
Sodium	153 milligrams

Exchanges
1/2 meat
1/4 starch

FRUIT AND CHEESE SPREAD

ingredients: 8 ounces nonfat cream cheese, softened
1 tbsp. nonfat sour cream
4 medium ripe bananas
1 tsp. lemon juice
1/4 cup raisins

directions: Mash bananas in a medium bowl and mix with lemon juice to prevent browning. Place banana mixture, cream cheese and sour cream in food processor or blender, and process until smooth and creamy. Fold in raisins; refrigerate.

Serves: 8

Nutrition per Serving

Calories	89
Carbohydrate	19 grams
Cholesterol	0 milligrams
Dietary Fiber	1 gram
Protein	4 grams
Sodium	180 milligrams

Exchanges

1 1/3 starch

GARLIC-CHEESE SPREAD

ingredients: 8 ounces nonfat cream cheese, softened
2 tbsp. skim milk
1 tsp. minced garlic
1/2 tsp. onion powder
2 tsp. red wine vinegar

directions: Place cream cheese in food processor or blender and process until smooth. Add milk, garlic, onion powder and vinegar, and process until ingredients are blended. Place mixture in bowl, cover, and refrigerate several hours before serving. Great on pita bread crisps or bagel chips.

Serves: 8

Nutrition per Serving

Calories	22
Carbohydrate	2 grams
Cholesterol	0 milligrams
Dietary Fiber	0 grams
Protein	4 grams
Sodium	179 milligrams

Exchanges

1/2 vegetable
1/4 meat

HERB SPREAD

ingredients: 2 cups nonfat cream cheese, softened
2 scallions, chopped fine
1 tsp. dried parsley
1/2 tsp. garlic powder
1/4 tsp. pepper
1/2 tsp. dried basil

directions: In a medium bowl, combine all ingredients and mix until well blended. Refrigerate several hours to blend flavors.

Serves: 10

Nutrition per Serving
Calories	39
Carbohydrate	3 grams
Cholesterol	0 milligrams
Dietary Fiber	0 grams
Protein	6 grams
Sodium	320 milligrams

Exchanges
2/3 meat
1/3 starch

HONEY-CHEESE SPREAD

ingredients: 6 ounces nonfat cream cheese, softened
1 tbsp. nonfat granola (almond flavor)
1 tbsp. honey
1/4 tsp. almond extract

directions: In a small bowl, combine cream cheese, granola honey and almond extract, and mix until blended. Refrigerate several hours or overnight.

Serves: 6

Nutrition per Serving
Calories	36
Carbohydrate	5 grams
Cholesterol	0 milligrams
Dietary Fiber	0 grams
Protein	4 grams
Sodium	177 milligrams

Exchanges
1/2 meat
1/3 starch

MUSTARD SAUCE

ingredients: 1 cup nonfat sour cream
1/2 tsp. mustard
1 tsp. horseradish

ingredients: Combine ingredients in small bowl and blend well. Refrigerate 1 to 2 hours before serving. Great with hot pretzels!

Serves: 4

Nutrition per Serving
Calories	42
Carbohydrate	< 1 gram
Cholesterol	0 milligrams
Dietary Fiber	0 grams
Protein	4 grams
Sodium	53 milligrams

Exchanges
1 meat

ORANGE-PINEAPPLE SPREAD

ingredients: 8 ounces nonfat cream cheese
4 tsp. skim milk
1/4 cup orange-pineapple marmalade

directions: Combine all ingredients in a food processor or blender and process until smooth. Refrigerate several hours or overnight.

Serves: 6

Nutrition per Serving

Calories	66
Carbohydrate	12 grams
Cholesterol	0 milligrams
Dietary Fiber	< 1 gram
Protein	5 grams
Sodium	239 milligrams

Exchanges

2/3 fruit
1/2 meat

PEACH BUTTER

ingredients: 1 cup dried peaches
16 ounces peach slices in light syrup
1/8 tsp. nutmeg
1/8 tsp. cinnamon

directions: Place dried peaches, canned peaches, cinnamon and nutmeg in a saucepan over medium heat. Bring mixture to a boil; reduce heat to low and simmer about 15 minutes, until almost all of the liquid has evaporated. Cool mixture; purée in food processor or blender, and refrigerate.

Serves: 8

Nutrition per Serving
Calories	79
Carbohydrate	21 grams
Cholesterol	0 milligrams
Dietary Fiber	2 grams
Protein	1 gram
Sodium	4 milligrams

Exchanges

1 1/2 fruit

PEACH SPICE BUTTER

ingredients: 8 cups peaches, peeled and sliced
1/2 cup frozen apple juice concentrate
1 cup water
1 1/2 tsp. cinnamon

directions: Place all ingredients in a medium saucepan over medium-high heat and bring mixture to a boil. Reduce heat to low and simmer, uncovered, 15 minutes. Remove from heat and cool. Place mixture in blender or food processor and purée until smooth; refrigerate.

Serves: 12

Nutrition per Serving

Calories	67
Carbohydrate	18 grams
Cholesterol	0 milligrams
Dietary Fiber	2 grams
Protein	< 1 gram
Sodium	3 milligrams

Exchanges

1 fruit

PINEAPPLE SPREAD

ingredients: 6 ounces nonfat cream cheese, softened
1/2 cup crushed pineapple in juice, drained
2 tsp. horseradish

directions: Combine all ingredients in a small bowl and mix until blended. Refrigerate several hours before serving.

Serves: 4

Nutrition per Serving

Calories	34
Carbohydrate	3 grams
Cholesterol	0 milligrams
Dietary Fiber	< 1 gram
Protein	5 grams
Sodium	293 milligrams

Exchanges

1/4 fruit
2/3 meat

PRUNE PURÉE

ingredients: 1 1/3 cups (8 ounces) pitted prunes
6 tbsp. hot water

directions: Combine prunes and hot water in a blender or food processor and process until smooth. Keeps refrigerated, for up to 2 months.

Yields: 1 cup

Nutrition per Serving

Calories	43
Carbohydrate	11 grams
Cholesterol	0 milligrams
Dietary Fiber	1 gram
Protein	< 1 gram
Sodium	< 1 milligram

Exchanges

2/3 fruit

SALMON-CHEESE SPREAD

ingredients: 1 1/2 cups nonfat cottage cheese
2 tbsp. lemon juice
2 tsp. Dijon mustard
1 tsp. prepared horseradish
4 ounces smoked salmon, diced

directions: Place all ingredients except salmon in food processor or blender and process until smooth. Fold in salmon and refrigerate 2 to 3 hours or overnight.

Serves: 6

Nutrition per Serving

Calories	33
Carbohydrate	1 gram
Cholesterol	5 milligrams
Dietary Fiber	0 grams
Protein	5 grams
Sodium	226 milligrams

Exchanges

1 meat

SALMON SPREAD

ingredients: 8 ounces nonfat cream cheese, softened
1 1/4 tsp. lemon juice
3 ounces smoked salmon
1 1/2 tbsp. chopped red onions
1 tsp. dill

directions: Combine all ingredients in a medium bowl and refrigerate several hours or overnight before serving.

Serves: 8

Nutrition per Serving

Calories	38
Carbohydrate	2 grams
Cholesterol	3 milligrams
Dietary Fiber	< 1 gram
Protein	6 grams
Sodium	226 milligrams

Exchanges

2/3 meat
1/2 vegetable

SMOKED SALMON SPREAD

ingredients: 4 ounces smoked salmon
5 tbsp. nonfat cream cheese
8 ounces nonfat cream cheese, softened
1/4 tsp. garlic powder
1/4 tsp. onion powder
1/8 tsp. pepper

directions: Place all ingredients in blender or food processor and process until smooth. Refrigerate several hours or overnight before serving.

Serves: 10

Nutrition per Serving
Calories	34
Carbohydrate	2 grams
Cholesterol	2 milligrams
Dietary Fiber	0 grams
Protein	5 grams
Sodium	225 milligrams

Exchanges
1/2 vegetable
1/2 meat

STRAWBERRY CHEESE SPREAD

ingredients: 8 ounces nonfat cream cheese, softened
2 tsp. nonfat sour cream
2 tsp. skim milk
1/3 cup frozen strawberries, thawed and chopped

directions: Place cream cheese, sour cream and milk in food processor or blender and process until smooth. Fold in chopped strawberries and mix well. Refrigerate several hours or overnight.

Serves: 8

Nutrition per Serving

Calories	24
Carbohydrate	2 grams
Cholesterol	0 milligrams
Dietary Fiber	< 1 gram
Protein	4 grams
Sodium	179 milligrams

Exchanges

1/3 milk

VEGGIE SPREAD

ingredients:
8 ounces nonfat cream cheese, softened
1/2 cup nonfat sour cream
1 tbsp. skim milk
1 tsp. onion powder
1/2 tsp. garlic powder
2 tbsp. red pepper, chopped
2 tbsp. carrots, grated
1 tbsp. cucumber, chopped
1 tbsp. scallion, chopped
1/3 tsp. Worcestershire sauce

directions:
In a medium bowl, combine cream cheese, sour cream, milk, onion powder, garlic powder and red pepper, and mix until blended smooth. Fold in chopped and grated vegetables and mix well. Refrigerate 2 to 3 hours or overnight.

Serves: 8

Nutrition per Serving
Calories	35
Carbohydrate	3 grams
Cholesterol	< 1 milligram
Dietary Fiber	< 1 gram
Protein	5 grams
Sodium	191 milligrams

Exchanges
1/2 vegetable
1/2 meat

FAT FREE LIVING 1
15202 North 50th Place • Scottsdale, Arizona 85254 • (602) 996-6300

Please send me _____ copies of your cookbook at $14.95 each plus $4.00 for postage , sales tax, and handling. Enclosed is my check payable to FAT FREE LIVING for $_____.

Name _____

Address _____

City _____ State _____ Zip _____

- -

FAT FREE LIVING 2
15202 North 50th Place • Scottsdale, Arizona 85254 • (602) 996-6300

Please send me _____ copies of your cookbook at $15.95 each plus $4.00 for postage , sales tax, and handling. Enclosed is my check payable to FAT FREE LIVING for $_____.

Name _____

Address _____

City _____ State _____ Zip _____

- -

FAT FREE LIVING 3 Desserts
15202 North 50th Place • Scottsdale, Arizona 85254 • (602) 996-6300

Please send me _____ copies of your cookbook at $15.95 each plus $4.00 for postage , sales tax, and handling. Enclosed is my check payable to FAT FREE LIVING for $_____.

Name _____

Address _____

City _____ State _____ Zip _____

- -

FAT FREE LIVING 4 Breads
15202 North 50th Place • Scottsdale, Arizona 85254 • (602) 996-6300

Please send me _____ copies of your cookbook at $14.95 each plus $5.00 for postage , sales tax, and handling. Enclosed is my check payable to FAT FREE LIVING for $_____.

Name _____

Address _____

City _____ State _____ Zip _____

- -

More FAT FREE Recipes

Share your fat-free recipes with the rest of the world! If you have a fat-free recipe that you feel belongs in <u>Recipes For FAT FREE LIVING 5</u>, please send it to me.

Jyl Steinback
Recipe for FAT FREE LIVING
15202 North 50th Place
Scottsdale, Arizona 85254
(602) 996-6300

We will make sure that you get credited for your contribution, with your name appearing on the page with your recipe. You will also receive a free copy of <u>Recipes for FAT FREE LIVING 4</u> when published.

So please state your name, address and telephone number, with signature under your recipe.

You may also contact me at the above address for speaking engagements or information about FAT FREE LIVING, Inc.

Love you lots,

And thanks for all your positive feedback! I appreciate YOU!

Jyl Steinback

Jyl Steinback

Index